SpringerBriefs in Computer Science

SpringerBriefs present concise summaries of cutting-edge research and practical applications across a wide spectrum of fields. Featuring compact volumes of 50 to 125 pages, the series covers a range of content from professional to academic.

Typical topics might include:

- A timely report of state-of-the art analytical techniques
- A bridge between new research results, as published in journal articles, and a contextual literature review
- A snapshot of a hot or emerging topic
- An in-depth case study or clinical example
- A presentation of core concepts that students must understand in order to make independent contributions

Briefs allow authors to present their ideas and readers to absorb them with minimal time investment. Briefs will be published as part of Springer's eBook collection, with millions of users worldwide. In addition, Briefs will be available for individual print and electronic purchase. Briefs are characterized by fast, global electronic dissemination, standard publishing contracts, easy-to-use manuscript preparation and formatting guidelines, and expedited production schedules. We aim for publication 8–12 weeks after acceptance. Both solicited and unsolicited manuscripts are considered for publication in this series.

**Indexing: This series is indexed in Scopus, Ei-Compendex, and zbMATH **

Patrick Brézillon

Research on Modeling and Using Context Over 25 Years

 Springer

Patrick Brézillon
LIP6
Sorbonne University
Paris, France

ISSN 2191-5768 ISSN 2191-5776 (electronic)
SpringerBriefs in Computer Science
ISBN 978-3-031-39337-2 ISBN 978-3-031-39338-9 (eBook)
https://doi.org/10.1007/978-3-031-39338-9

This Springer imprint is published by the registered company Springer Nature Switzerland AG
The registered company address is: Gewerbestrasse 11, 6330 Cham, Switzerland

Preface

In the play "Le bourgeois gentilhomme" (1670), Molière makes fun of a wealthy bourgeois who wants to imitate the behavior and way of life of the nobles. The gentleman calls on a teacher to develop his general knowledge in order to shine in society and discovers that he was using prose with his everyday words. This revelation makes the gentleman very proud of this knowledge. In some ways, we all are the Mr. Jourdain of context because context is an intrinsic part of our life, of our objectives, reasoning and actions, of the situation we are in and the local environment where the required resources are. However, we all have different views on context. During the research on modeling context, 249 definitions were found (up to 2023). It is a weakness for communication, especially interdisciplinary communication. It also is a challenge that has been met with success in the research presented in this monograph with the animation of the international and interdisciplinary community interested by the modeling and use of context, and the organization of the series of biannual conferences from CONTEXT-97 (Rio de Janeiro, Brazil) to CONTEXT-19 (Trento, Italy).

Working on a wide range of applications was a strength for attacking the modeling and use of context because each application puts an emphasis only on some specific aspects of context, and the results of the modeling of context on this particular application are directly applicable in other applications as a side effect, often leading to highlight in other applications some aspects of the domain initially not considered.

At a more conceptual level, such a modeling of context leads to some unexpected views on some topics normally relating more to purely theoretical approaches like contextual reasoning, decision-making, diagnosis, problem solving or cognitive approaches where general concepts like mental model and mental representation do not always arrive to an operational expression. For example, in decision-making, it is not the result that is the most important, but the process leading to this result because this process is context-dependent.

This monograph presents the main results of research during 25 years on modeling and using context in real-world applications in a very large spectrum of domains, like power systems, Control and Command systems, psychology and medicine. The examples used in the monograph come from six of those applications for illustrating the aspects of context put frontstage. However, the approach followed in this research is not limited to a sketch of what a model of context could be, but the approach covers the conceptual and operational levels as far as a software is implemented and used in all the applications presented, with the exception of the first application for Electricité de France which served as a trigger for this research.

Indeed, the first findings of the research pointed out the originality of the approach with respect to the other studies at that time. Clearly, one cannot speak of context in an abstract way. Context can be understood only through its relationships with knowledge and reasoning in real-world applications; that is, context can be modeled with knowledge and reasoning in a uniform representation based on a bottom-up approach. However, this does not mean that context must be modeled specifically only for each application. Indeed, it is fascinating to see that the resulting piece of software, the contextual graphs, relies on a handful of items, which makes the software very easy to use (training of 15 mn) by students in domains far from computer science and AI (e.g. psychology, medicine, lawyer). The twenty-two other key points identified all along the presentation are synthetized and discussed in a last section. These key milestones rely on an operational definition of context that opened up a conceptual framework associated with an implementation framework, the Contextual Graphs (CxG) formalism.

A second challenge was the application of the CxG formalism from one actor realizing a task to a group of actors realizing an activity. The transition from one actor to N actors necessitated an evolution of the conceptual approach to replace the contextualized task model identified for one actor to a new modeling of each user task in terms of elementary independent subtask for representing an activity as the execution of a subtask sequence, that is, the dynamic building of the initial contextualized task model. The change of view on a task realization (for one actor) to an activity (for N actors) allows the introduction of the notion of shared context equally built during the activity for representing the exchanges of contextual information between the actors. What is interesting is that it was not a bifurcation point because the task realization by an actor also can be modeled in the second version of the CxG formalism, going from an external viewpoint on the task realization in the first CxG version to an internal viewpoint in the second CxG version. This transition enriches the modeling of the task realization/activity by making context management explicit with the group activity development. Making context explicit leads to deep simplifications of the modeling of artificial or living systems because the resulting framework covers the strong connections between context and, on the one hand, the focus of attention of the actor(s) and, on the other hand, knowledge and reasoning.

The research presentation also sheds new light on the decisional levels, namely policy, strategy, tactics and operations. Context allows to distinguish a conceptual level and an operational one, context intervening mainly at the second level without rejecting the fact that there are contextual elements of the first group that may have a more direct role on the focus of attention than contextual elements closer of the focus. The proposal of the onion metaphor is particularly relevant for showing the links between context and decisional levels.

The CxG formalism allows the use of context models of a task realization in AI systems (because AI systems are not limited to algorithms), but can rely on bases of experience like the contextual graphs. The bottom-up approach does not lead to discovery as deep learning, but a possibility would be to use the sum of the bases of experiences developed in a domain (concerning all the tasks to realize in the domain) as a support for a "glocal" (global and local) learning on the domain. Some elements are identified for designing and implementing context-based intelligent assistant systems.

Beyond the applications used for modeling and use context, the conceptual framework also has been used for providing an alternative explanation of applications realized by other researchers. The semiotics approach, which was used for interpreting the attempts made for transferring the Walt Disney Company at internationalization, is revisited with the concept of contextualization-decontextualization-recontextualization presented in the monograph. In return, the model of the sign, signified and signifier opens the door for an interesting representation (and understanding) of the concepts of contextual element and instantiation. The comparison of notion of mental model and mental representation in cognitive science and of practice and contextual graph lead to improve the notions in their respective domains. There are also several past modelings, like the hierarchical task analysis and breast cancer diagnosis, that are presented in a simple and evolutive way as contextual graphs.

The last but not the least point to say in this preface concerns thanks to too numerous persons (about 150) that participated in this successful adventure. I would like to thank two special persons, Juliette et Céline, enthusiastic and active supporters of their father with the development of a robust shared context distributed on different media, especially in difficult times, their participation in the organization of the two CONTEXT conferences, on their appropriation of the CxG formalism, one in her master's dissertation (for modeling the revocation of the Edict of Nantes in a contextual graph) and the other, in her Ph.D. thesis (for a context-based intelligent tutorial system for the self-evaluation of drivers' behavior). Now, after, I hope to collaborate with researchers to continue this exciting adventure.

Paris, France   Patrick Brézillon

Contents

Chapter 1
Introduction

This paper is an attempt for synthetizing 25 years of research on the modeling of context and its use in about 20 real-world project and applications.[1] The topic "Modeling and using context" is found in a number of disciplines either directly (i.e. as context) or indirectly (i.e. like situations, constraints, etc.). Our objective is not to make a thorough study of the literature in all the disciplines, especially in disciplines, where old references (say, 1940) are stable since a long time and remain quoted. Most of the references cited in this paper come from artificial intelligence (AI) and computer science and some related disciplines.

It was not possible to have a linear line of reasoning during the 25 years. It was rather a "broken line" of reasoning often pushed by intuitions (justified a posteriori) and by the applications that were like points of bifurcations in the reasoning because each application has context specificities put frontstage (e.g. a voting system in group activity) that appeared, consequently, as an additional benefit in other applications.

Indeed, the research has been successful thanks to the challenges brought by the "real-world" projects and applications which prohibited arbitrary simplification for modeling context. Our interest in decision-making led us to establish an operational definition of context. It was then possible to really model context in terms that had a concrete meaning for actors with whom we collaborated in very different domains. In this paper, we briefly presented six of the projects and applications on which we worked for an illustrative purpose.

Another constraint on our survey of the literature is the rapid evolution of Information and Communication Technology (ICT) since the eighties. The half-life duration of references judged important is very long in some disciplines existing before 1980 (literature, for sure, but also in disciplines concerning more the human than the machine) and very short in other disciplines, like our disciplines—AI and computer

---

[1] The list of the publications (and PDF for most of them) of the projects and applications is given at http://www-poleia.lip6.fr/%7Ebrezil/Pages2/Publications/index.html (ask the author for PDF not on the website or after 2017).

© The Author(s), under exclusive license to Springer Nature Switzerland AG 2023
P. Brézillon, *Research on Modeling and Using Context Over 25 Years*,
SpringerBriefs in Computer Science,
https://doi.org/10.1007/978-3-031-39338-9_1

sciences—but also recent disciplines such as management. It implies a large gap between what the access to the published scientific literature was before and since ICT, especially if the digitization of old books has not been made. Moreover, sciences introduce new concepts (e.g. data processing) and require an assimilation or accommodation of past concepts, if not obsolete. In a sense, accounting for ICT evolution supposes to reinvent the wheel in the scientific literature.

Several concepts like task, task realization, procedure, practice, different types of context, etc. are used in this book in the same or different ways of other disciplines. The research that is the core of this book was led in artificial intelligence (AI) from the modeling of task realization, decision-making and problem solving that we sum up as "focus of attention" for the generic aspects of context. AI is a discipline between "hard sciences", where a theorem proven in 1922 stays valid now because it was made in a hypothesis of "closed world", but "soft sciences" faces life in "open-world" conditions and where any finding can be called into question any time. Following the ICT revolution, especially with the web, the life duration of publications is 5–10 years, which does not question some old publications (e.g. some tests in neuropsychiatry established in 1975 are always used for evaluating the memory capacity of patients nowadays, 2023, in a radically different context). The research presented in this book has been the object of numerous papers published in different journals, reviews and conferences; thus, we will not enter in all the details of the results obtained, and later another book will cover these research details. In this book, we limit the research presentation to what is strictly necessary for a coherent view on the evolution our research on modeling and use of context and on the main general lessons learned in our research.

Our objective is to propose a formalization for approaching the concept of context from an AI viewpoint—like the concepts of mass, length, speed, etc. in Physics and Biology—for modeling how an actor or a group of actors realize a task in real-world applications. Modeling context for a given focus like task realization, decision-making and problem solving supposes to clearly establish its close relationships with human knowledge and reasoning that are used in real-world applications. The midterm goal of our context modeling is to establish a pragmatic approach to design, develop and implement context-based AI systems that rely on the operational knowledge used by humans in relationships with any focus of attention. Making context explicit allows to use humans' experience that encompasses the nature of the task, the situation in which the task must be realized and available means in environment that are necessary for that. Human, task, situation and environment are strongly intertwined, and context includes the expression of the whole.

What is context? An annual count of the number of web pages containing the word "context" showed fifteen years ago an exponential increase from 650,000 in 1996 to 325,000,000 pages in 2006 (after 2006, Google filtered unused web pages). About 90% of the pages were not relevant for our purpose of modeling context (e.g. containing "…in this context, we think that…"). Nevertheless, the number of relevant pages was heightened by 500 over these ten years. If it was possible at that time to make an interdisciplinary survey of the literature (e.g. see [1]), rapidly a survey only was possible at the level of each discipline. The situation was aggravated by the move of bibliographic references from paper support to digital ones. The consequence was that references had "to be on the Web or to do not exist" in most of the disciplines, and the corollary is the lack of accessibility of the old publications judged as "THE" references in some disciplines (especially books). With respect to our research, the bibliography we made is mainly on what is accessible on the web and not on what is on paper, especially in other disciplines.

Which definition of context? Bazire and Brézillon [2] have analyzed 166 definitions of context (249 definitions in 2023) in more than thirty disciplines. Here are some examples in six different disciplines:

- A collection of relevant conditions and surrounding influences that make *a situation* unique and comprehensible (AI);
- The set of all entities which influence *human cognitive behavior* on a particular occasion (cognitive science);
- What surrounds and gives meaning to *something* (linguistic);
- A body of information available to participants in the *speech situation* (philosophy);
- The social relations and structures in a larger scale situation, *the situation* being defined by the population, equipment, spatial and temporal elements (organizational science);
- As the fibers of a rope for describing the conditions of a *system* (sociology).

The underlined words in the definitions above correspond to the focus of attention that is concerned by the context in the definition. Some immediate observations can be made: (1) It seems to exist as many definitions as authors (and sometimes several definitions by author); (2) few definitions allow to make context operational; (3) a definition is given in terms of the discipline (i.e. highly contextualized); and (4) even if definitions are contextualized, some generic features emerge, linking context to a focus of attention.

Why do we need context? The need of context appears as soon as humans and their activities intervene. We have not considered the intellectual and theoretical activities, only activities with an operational purpose (especially modeling and simulation for reasoning modeling). When humans realize a task, make decision, solve a problem in the real world, they adapt methods, tools, etc. during the process to take into account the constraints of the task, the situation, the environment and also their preferences, emotions, etc., that is, the context of the human reasoning. Our question then is how an AI system can use effectively context for exploiting the human's knowledge and reasoning put in the machine without enumerating all the contextual variants. This supposes a uniform representation of knowledge, reasoning and context and an efficient software for modeling the human focus of attention in context. In all our projects and applications for large (and small) enterprises, the human that we considered is the actor that has a focus on a task, a decision or a problem.

We develop the presentation of our research in the following way.

Chapter 2 gives the needed presentation of the projects and applications which are catalysts in our research, and all the examples given in the following sections are taken in these applications.

Chapter 3 shows that context is intertwined with operational knowledge and reasoning in real-world applications (particularly in domains where knowledge occurs in an operational form that is different of knowledge represented in formal models).

Chapter 4 presents the main points on the modeling of context for its use by an actor in real-world applications from the conceptual aspects, the operational aspects and the context-based formalism of representation called contextual graphs (CxG).

Chapter 5 discusses which natural extension of the research presented in the previous section was necessary for modeling context associated with the focus of a group of actors, from conceptual and operational aspect of context as well as for the CxG formalism.

Chapter 6 gathers the lessons learned (identified as key points in the previous chapters) that pointed out all along the book in a general discussion leading the basis of context-based intelligent assistant systems.

Finally, the conclusion shows that this 25-year research is not the last page of the story but opens the door on new horizons.

We want to give right now a working definition of context to understand this chapter: "Context is defined as a set of contextual elements that do not appear explicitly in the focus of attention". The origins of the real definition are given in Chap. 3, and the operational definition and the consequences are then explained in detail in Chap. 4.

References

1. Brézillon, P.: Context in problem solving: a survey. Knowl. Eng. Rev. **14**(1), 1–34 (1999)
2. Bazire, M., Brézilon, P.: Understanding context before to use it. In: Dey, A., et al. (eds.) CONTEXT-05: Modeling and Using Context. Lecture Notes in Artificial Intelligence, vol. 3554, pp. 29–40. Springer Verlag (2005)

Chapter 2
The Real-World Applications

The research relies on several real-world applications since 25 years in a very large spectrum of domains: power systems, subway exploitation, enology with wine-making, computer security, collaborative understanding, car driver support, web site analysis, self-training of car drivers, medical image access, contextualization of platforms of interoperable open-source tools for enterprises, database administration, strategic infrastructure project in transportation, cognition-driven explorer for histopathology for breast cancer grading, process and sharing of medical images and contextualized support on a tablet for a Control and Command system for French military.

This chapter gives a brief presentation of six of them in which the examples given in this book are drawn to illustrate the aspects of context put frontstage: SEPT (1986–1995), SART (1996–2002), FlexMIm (2012–2015), TACTIC (2013–2015), "Prediction of the stuck of wine fermentations" (1997–1999) and the project "Computer-mediated collaborative work" (1997–1999).

2.1 The SEPT Project (1986–1995)

The project "Surveillance d'Equipements dans les Poste à très haute Tension" (SEPT) concerned the equipment monitoring in Extra High Voltage (EHV, 400,000 V) substations [1]. An automated control system monitors a system and automatically eliminates faults, but such control systems are themselves subject to failures. SEPT examines both systems to give two kind of outputs, namely a synthetic diagnostic conclusion and a model-based explanation.

When a fault appears on the network, a whole set of control systems "sees" the fault and react. Thus, there is an avalanche of signals arriving at the status logger for a very short period of time (usually 1–2 s), with problems such as telescoping of signals (simultaneity of two signals which results in only one being recorded on the status logger). Normally, only the control systems, which directly supervise the element of the network supporting the fault, must open.

The diagnosis of equipment failures (or inconsistency between the operation of two devices) is carried out by analyzing the operation of the equipment during fault elimination (controllers can emit 100 signal events). The diagnosis is realized by comparing the logical sequence of events and the real sequence of events which have occurred: at the level of each device, at the level of the devices in a control system and at the level of the EHV substation. The offline diagnosis of automated control systems has two special features:

- Reasoning concerns the overall system (both the controlled system and the control system).
- Many redundant observations must be analyzed rapidly to identify an abnormal behavior in the control system.

The SEPT project was a 9-year experiment. SEPT has been in operation in September 1990. It was able to cover several power substations, each comprising 15 power lines, four busbar sections and two transformers. However, three expert systems finally have been developed: a diagnostician (the SEPT expert system), a simulator and a knowledge configurator.

SEPT was written in a production rules formalism based on the logic of first-order predicates using an expert systems generator developed at EDF. It was coupled with a simulator for an exhaustive theoretical validation of SEPT because incidents on the power system are rare and of very short duration (and corrections must be made rapidly). The diagnostician and simulator were initially designed from technical manuals. Without altering the knowledge base, the diagnostic tool successfully resolved the whole set of incidents that occurred in EHV substations of different topologies.

After the theoretical validation by the simulator, EDF carried out a pragmatic validation on site in an EHV substation in the north of the Paris region. The version of SEPT installed in this workstation was running in parallel with the usual human operations in the EHV substation (SEPT was supplied directly by the data found on the status logger, and the workstation topology at the time of the problem was provided by another software). The operators of this EHV substation then checked the diagnosis of SEPT in relation to their own diagnosis. After a year, it was possible to correct some minor errors in SEPT. The first real-size validation in an EHV substation was a success (the expert system also diagnosed equipment failures not detected by operators).

On the strength of these two validations, EDF then decided to begin a gradual installation of the expert system in all EHV substations in France, starting with a substation in the Alps which had very different characteristics from the substation in the Paris region. Rapidly, it became obvious that it was not question of porting the SEPT expert system without modifications so far-reaching that a rewrite of SEPT appeared mandatory.

Indeed, although domain knowledge about equipment is the same in all EHV substations, the contexts in which this knowledge was used were very different. For example, in the mountains it is not possible to space the equipment as in the plains. This had consequences on the way in which the information was repatriated to the status logger (e.g. the "fallout" of information was not recorded, while part of the diagnosis of SEPT essentially depended on this information). Other reasons also existed: Only the operation of official equipment was recorded, certain equipment not approved by the company was used (and the expertise was not in SEPT), etc.

As a consequence, a third step of the research concerned a knowledge configurator for tailoring the SEPT expert system to specificity of each EHV substation. (In terms used nowadays, the knowledge configurator would be called "contextualizator".) The knowledge configurator KA7 ("Knowledge Acquisition for SEPT") system aims to develop specific clones of SEPT for each EHV substation, which are adapted to specific environments (topologies, equipment on the site, adaptation of "EDF rules" to the current context, etc.), because if all EHV substations are supposed to perform the same task, they are in different contexts, one by the sea and the other in the high mountains. Thus, it was important to contextualize the clones of SEPT.

However, the SEPT representation presented other weaknesses, the main one being an artificial knowledge structuring (mainly knowledge on the topology of the electrical network) based on screening clauses to handle procedural knowledge in a declarative language. The initial rule-based formalism of production has been modified, first to support explicitly the structure of domain knowledge in the form of independent rule packets for equipment pieces [2] and second the possibility of simulating the behavior of the diagnostician in different contexts to get explanations at different levels of detail. An explanation provides contextual information which is not necessary for the diagnosis, but conditions this diagnosis.

There is other contextual information which was kept more deeply implicit (because it was obvious for experts) such as the fact that equipment pieces work only as long as the fault is seen on the network (control equipment stop functioning when the fault disappears).

The SEPT project highlighted that a real modeling of context was missing. First, the lack of possibility to represent quantitative domain knowledge with the qualitative nature of rule-based representation obliged us to introduce screening clauses and rule-packet management instead of a real modeling of context. This situation occurred often for other expert systems at that time. Second, because the SEPT expert system was established for a "decontextualized" EHV substation (a theoretical model or task model as said in the following), a knowledge configurator was implemented for "contextualizing" the SEPT expert system for each particular EHV substation.

If the SEPT project would be revisited, we will put context at the core of the knowledge (instead of screening clauses and rule packets) and reasoning (instead of control knowledge in the inference engine) representation. This has been done in the following project for the subway in Paris (France) and Rio de Janeiro (Brazil).

2.2 The SART Project (1996–2002)

The SART project (SART stands for "Système d'Aide à la Régulation du Trafic", French acronym of support system for traffic control, [3, 4]) aimed at developing an intelligent decision support system to help the operators who control a subway line to react to incidents that occur on the line.

Incident management on a subway line is a difficult task mainly for two reasons. First, a global strategy of the company is to rapidly return to a normal operating mode, and this strategy concerns any incident solving. Second, when an incident occurs, there are numerous parameters that intervene coming from several heterogeneous sources. All the operators, which all monitor their lines in a unique control room, have just a few minutes (or seconds) when an incident occurs to analyze the situation, collect contextual information, identify the context in which the incident occurred and make decision.

The Parisian subway company RATP faces daily incidents since 1900. For the sake of security and incident-solving standardization, the company head established secure procedures for each type of incident. For example, the procedure for the incident "ill traveler on a train" instructs the driver to stop the next station because it is easier to assure the security of passengers at a station rather than in a tunnel. At a deeper level, the driver must avoid stopping the train for a long time in a tunnel because some passengers may have behavioral troubles such as claustrophobia and could try to leave the train (and thus generate another incident such as "passenger on the tracks").

A procedure is a safe action sequence that is supposed to solve an incident in any situation or context and mainly relies on the natural structure of the domain knowledge. This decontextualization by abstraction leads to robust procedures that cover a large range of similar incident-solving procedures but, as a counter-effect, often results in suboptimal solutions. As a consequence, operators adapt procedures as useful guidelines (more or less officially) for each new incident that occurs [5]. They do not rely on standard procedures because (a) the standard procedure is rarely well-adapted to the situation at hand and could lead to improper actions or suboptimal incident-solving strategies, and (b) a standard procedure may cause the operator to miss important information or lead them to noticing them too late to adequately solve the incident.

Many operators prefer to plan their actions in real time and develop *practices* based on a use-oriented organization of the domain knowledge and on their experience. Thus, procedures serve as frames to construct strategies tailored to a given situation's specificity and to develop practices (the assembling of actions in a sequence performed to treat a particular incident in its context) by contextualizing the procedure.

For example, a procedure may preconize to stop the train at a station, but if the station is a connection with another subway line, there is a danger of a massive influx of travelers willing to get on the train at the station. This is generally built up case by case and complemented with "makeshift repairs" that allow the operators to reach the required efficiency. It is a way to achieve the result no matter the path followed. However, this part of the operational knowledge is not captured in procedures.

Operators give a great importance to contextual knowledge (e.g. it is rush hour) for monitoring subway lines in the situation of an incident. An operator said us, "when I am informed of an incident on my line, I first look to the current state of the whole line to gather contextual information" and then make decision accordingly. Landauer and Bellman [6] similarly conclude that the process of problem solving presents three major steps: "find_context", "pose_problem" and "study_problem". Context includes information and knowledge on the situation that do not intervene directly in the incident solving (e.g. it is rush hour), but constrain the way in which the operator will choose a strategy (e.g. choose the faster way) at each step of the incident solving.

To identifying situation's specificity, operators elaborate a scenario (a sequence of actions intertwined with events that do not depend on operators but constrain their actions) based on contextual knowledge and postpone actions in order to quickly make decision after first collect and analyze a maximum of contextual information. Such a look-ahead reasoning reduces the scenario's uncertainty and gives an idea of the best strategy to apply. Scenario building corresponds to the proceduralization of a part of the contextual knowledge that operators will make operational to assemble actions in a sequence. Built scenarios enable access to common intermediary situations as they can reuse common strategies to solve the incident. Consequently, some common action sequences exist in different practices.

Operators contextualize their operational knowledge and store it in an adapted computational structure, which will be easily understood by other operators and efficiently used by computer systems. The subway-traffic regulation requires the control of a huge quantity of knowledge pieces more or less implicit in the regulation itself. Experience shows that the consequences of an incident are highly dependent on the context in which the incident occurs (e.g. rush hours or not).

The SART system was designed and implemented for helping operators and train driver facing an incident to find rapidly the right procedure to apply. We first develop a rule-based system for representing the official procedures. However, this representation was rejected by operators because it was illegible (too important redundancy), and the representation did not consider the contextual variants of the procedures [7].

We then translate the rule-based representation in a decision tree representation. There was a better acceptance of the representation by operators, but we (designer and developer) faced a representation too difficult to manage, especially when the addition of a new practice led to doubling the number of branches of the decision tree.

Finally, a new transformation of the decision tree into a graph representation was the right solution for controlling the development of the graph and for introducing *contextual elements* instead of "chance nodes". The contextual graph representation formalism (see Sect. 4.3) was born and after used in practically all our projects and applications.

2.3   The FlexMIm Project (2012–2015)

The FlexMIm project (French acronym for "Platform for processing and sharing medical images in a cloud environment: adaptation to anatomo-pathology") focused on the formalization of medical practices in chronic inflammatory bowel disease (IBD) diagnosis. The consortium comprised two large enterprises, four research laboratories and 27 experts. It was an important concern of anatomo-cyto-pathologists (ACPs) in a decreasing professional population facing an increasing number of acts.

Anatomical Pathology (AP) concerns the macroscopic and microscopic examination of patients' tissue samples and cells in order to establish the diagnosis and the factors of severity of the disease. ACPs follow procedures that include a gross examination (visual examination of organs), dissection and sampling of surgical specimens according to standardized protocols and then a microscopic examination of stained tissue sections.

The FlexMIm project aimed to provide ACPs a platform for their collaborative work (initial diagnosis, tele-expertise, remote learning) based on the technology of "digital slides" (the images view in a microscope is scanned in 30-Go files and used instead of the "real slides"). Digital slides have the advantage of allowing relocation of reading and collaborative work, but their processing is yet to establish. Our work concerned the modeling of ACPs' reasoning during IBD diagnosis from analysis of digital images as a contextual graph to identify a consensual methodology [8].

Anatomical Pathology aims to examine macroscopically, but also microscopically, patients' tissue samples and cells in order to establish not only the diagnosis but also the factors of severity of the tumor, contributing thus to therapeutic decisions.

For that, the ACP physicians have procedures that include a gross examination (visual examination of diseased tissues), dissection and sampling of surgical specimens according to well-defined protocols and then a microscopic examination of stained tissue sections. The ACP's diagnosis is based on normal anatomy, histology and cytology to identify, by analogy, macroscopic and microscopic morphological abnormalities. It also uses several techniques such as immuno-histochemistry, cytogenetic and molecular biology to identify molecular abnormalities in cells or tissues.

Beyond this large spectrum of data, information and knowledge about the problem, there are the intervention of external elements like the type of task to accomplish, the actor realizing the task, the situation in which the task is realized and the available resources in the immediate environment. Such contextual elements may impact deeply the task realization. If they are not integrated in the reasoning, this could lead to nonconformity.

The main goals of the FlexMIm project are:

1. To facilitate consultation of digital slides ensuring the quality of the scanned slides and pre-annotation of the regions of interest that can then be downloaded and/or pre-analyzed in priority;

2. To develop and implement a cognitive approach that will be integrated into hospital workflows between patients, pathological reports and image archiving system;
3. To identify regions of interest on digital slides;
4. To record manual annotations of ACPs for completing the automatic annotations.

Twenty-seven experts participated in the project to evaluate and validate the effectiveness of cooperative work processes and collaboration provided by the project centered on pathological imaging, leading to its ownership in its scale and spread after drafting a trade repository.

The knowledge acquisition phase and the modeling of the expertise were organized around three workshops about the choice of diseases to study, the observation of how pathologists worked, the identification of similarity in pathologists' works and the proposal of a unified view. The "knowledge manager" for our modeling was a physician knowing the expert knowledge used by ACPs but having not their expertise (she was medical intern at that time). Patient's data are collected during complex diagnostic decision-making and long-term treatment in oncology. They do not simply form a chronology of events, but they built up a network of various relationships between numerous information pieces. In the domain of cancer therapy, a single laboratory value, for example, is useless without knowing the previous values and the particular temporal context (e.g. chemotherapy or radiotherapy administered before or at the same time).

Our model of the IBD expertise as represented in the contextual graph is original under several aspects.

First, the contextual graph gives a unified view on different ways to diagnose dysplasia by different ACPs in a domain that is not formalized. Its validation by the 27 ACPs means that each ACP agrees on the representation of his/her expertise and accepts the expertise of the other ACPs. This validation was the opportunity for ACPs to establish a shared glossary. Thus, the contextual graph and the glossary constituted a shared *experience base.*

Second, the modeling of the *glocal search* is an important process of decision-making for them.

Third, the *voting system* is an alternative to formal approaches in decision-making because the vote process can be tailored to each ACP.

Fourth, experience sharing—knowledge as the glossary and reasoning as in the contextual graph—offers a new platform for an efficient collaborative decision-making. It is possible "to remember" details, explain and justify any step in the reasoning, the automatic generation of reports, the expert glossary accepted by all the actors and for the training of future actors because based on real work practices.

2.4   The TACTIC Project (2013–2015)

The objective of the TACTIC project (French acronym for "Contextualized support on a tablet for the transmission of command information", [9]) was the development of a man–machine interface on touchpad for a software of Command and Control (C2) for military, easy to use, that helps operators to manage the complexity of the commands and information at their disposal. Such information and communication systems give operators a view of the operational situation, typically with a map overlaid with symbols that represent (military) units. A C2 system gathers information from several sources and lets the actor communicate and give orders directly. Such systems also are used, or on the way to being used, by first responders or large operators in the private sector. Military C2 systems that are used on the field generally have a touch interface of small size to address the requirements of mobility and simplicity of use in difficult situations.

Up to now, interfaces were complex to use and required training. There are three zones on the interface. First, a geographical map as representation of the global situation for following events; second, the ODB (order of battle) as representation of the units and their activities; and, three, the event chronology as representation of the scenario and the actions responsible of the events.

The result of the TACTIC project was a mockup[1] of an intelligent interface on a tablet for a C2 system to handle commands. This interface takes advantage of all the possibilities of gestural touch interfaces to be able to effectively provide the information that applies to a broad spectrum of orders and to develop a cognitive man–machine interface that includes the context and history of use to enable actors to manage the complexity of the system.

Current touchscreen C2s have basic button-based interfaces that make manipulations complex and require good knowledge of the actor. The project proposed:

- To use the range of possibilities offered by tactile interfaces (multi-touch control, gestures) for an easy and efficient interface to use;
- To present interface behavior at any time with shortcuts and intelligent assistance in order to help it understand the complexity of the system.

The interface was integrated in a C2 system and a simulator that receives the order of the C2 system and sends reports on a realistic simulated operational situation that evolves depending on the messages coming from the operator, as a test and validation tool for the interface. The smart touch interface model explicitly incorporates the notion of context as contextual elements to present the actor with the most relevant commands and information at any time.

Our actors were nine experts of the company developing the battle simulator SWORD. Only one was military scientific consultant (considered as a strategic expert), and the civil experts had an expertise very close of those of the military experts. The two main classes of actors were tactical experts (project development

---

[1] The French army, our sponsor, asked for pragmatic ideas that they will implement alone.

manager, pre-sales project managers) and operational experts (modelers, quality manager), with thus two distinct focuses for interacting with the simulator SWORD in real conditions.

An interesting point of the TACTIC project was the modeling of the mental representations of experts (see Sect. 3.2 for our use of "representation" and "model"). First, we developed a domain model with 342 elements coming from different documents (as books and reports) in a classical type of task analysis [10]. This domain model was adjusted to the use of the simulator by experts, and finally only 105 contextual elements were selected for constituting a kind of generic mental representation. This provides experts with a starting point for express their personal mental representations as mental maps.[2] After, experts were put in real conditions for working with the simulator on a given scenario (reconnoiter of a situation). At the end of the session, experts were required to suppress the contextual elements of their mental representation they did not used during the session and thus establish the mental model corresponding to the scenario development, the decisions made and the actions taken.

The mental representation corresponds to the partially structured knowledge that experts used at least once during their work. This mental representation can move away of the domain model by a total reorganization of the elements that corresponds the best to the experts' reasoning during task realization. Each mental representation is personal and implies that experts realize the same task in different contexts from a same domain representation. Variants of the procedures appear as soon as it exists freedom degrees in the way to realize the task, including the use of tools.

The interface is a communication medium similar to a shared context through which the operator and the simulator interact via interface actions (currently, mapping, tabs, zooming, window management, etc.). Changing the interface (or using several ones) then obliges to ensure the conversion of the domain actions performed by the operator into those performed by the simulator and reciprocally. This approach opens the way to new graphic and gestural concepts for a new medium like the tablet. The interface between the actor and the simulator is "physical" but also "cognitive". It is an active intermediary for translating messages (information, order to execute) from human to the simulator and vice versa.

The lessons learned from the TACTIC project are threefold [11].

The first lesson concerns, at the physical interaction level, the differentiation of the actions of the operator and those of the simulator for the control of the simulation and finally the identification of the actions that are related to the interface. For example, by clicking on the pause button on the interface, the operator thinks to stop the simulation, while this action is transferred through the interface to the simulator that suspends the simulation. As a consequence, the operator associates the control of the simulation with actions on the interface that is supposed to play the role of the simulator for the operator. Operator–simulator interaction (cognitive

---

[2] Mental maps were built by experts with the software FreeMind.

interaction) is considered secondary to interaction with the interface (physical interaction). Indeed, operators in our experiment said to "interact with the simulation", not with the simulator because the simulation was the visible part of the combined work of the interface and the simulator.

The second lesson is to make compatible, at the level of the cognitive interaction, the operator's mental representation and the three sources of information of the simulator, say the "simulator's mental representation" (i.e. the geographical map, the ODB and the event chronology).

The third lesson is the importance to consider the interface as a full group member in a computer-mediated group activity (but not modeled in this study) with the operator and the simulator.

2.5   Wine-Making Project (1997–1999)

In this project, we addressed the critical problem of stops in the alcoholic fermentation and the difficulties that may rise in its achievement. Wine-making is a domain where formalization is very difficult (or even impossible), mainly because one has to deal with heterogeneous knowledge that comes into play at different steps of the wine-making process. Whatever the causes are, the consequence of a stop in alcoholic fermentation is the same: the fermentation process, in which sugar is transformed into alcohol, slows down (sometimes very much) or even stops completely, leaving too much sugar in the wine.

These events are respectively called sluggish and stuck fermentations. They can result in wine spoilage because there is a severe control on wine quality (e.g. for quality reasons, the final sugar concentration in the wine must be lower than 2 g/l, except for sweet wines).

Our contribution aimed to help wine-makers to predict a stop in the normal fermentation process as soon as possible. Several approaches already existed (e.g. neural networks, knowledge-based systems). However, these attempts failed to give a satisfactory solution mainly because they had a too partial view of the problem.

The fermentation step of the wine-making process is strongly correlated with events that occur at previous steps. The vine-growing is not directly related to the alcoholic fermentation, even if knowledge of the former step is used by the wine-maker in the latter step. We call such knowledge contextual knowledge, and our goal is to design and implement a contextual knowledge-based system.

The problem to solve (fermentation stops) is like the heart of an onion, and contextual knowledge is organized in layers around the heart in an order that relies on a qualitative distance. In the most frequent cases of blended fermentations, the good fermentative qualities of one wine variety can compensate for the faults of another. The consequences are lost money, full vats, critical time deadlines not respected and possible noxious effects [12].

Several actors intervene all along the process, the main ones being vine-grower, cellar master, enologist, the microbiologist and a laboratory. Each actor has his own working context different from that of others, but shared some knowledge with them. Our modeling of the problem had to account for all the types of knowledge, the ones concerning directly the fermentation as well as those as far away as the weather during vine-growing for example.

From the expert knowledge gathered from interviews, a model of the domain (deep knowledge) and a set of rules (shallow knowledge) have been implemented. A simulation from the model provides an evaluation of the risk of stuck fermentation of a particular must. Before the simulation, we have a set of data that leads a description of a must at the beginning of the fermentation phase or during it. We use all the available information about previous phases (measured chemical parameters, actions already done, etc.).

Unfortunately, it is not always possible (and almost never in the fermentation case) to derive an explicit path between contextual knowledge and the focus, mainly by lack of information that can correspond to a lack of communication between experts or by a too complex deep knowledge for being organized correctly. To overcome the problem, we first used shallow knowledge as contextual knowledge. The incomplete path is replaced by a global link between known pieces of knowledge and the focus in the spirit of the subgoaling in SOAR [13]. For example, some enologists use the following rule: if the vat's temperature is higher than 30 °C (for red wines) and if there is no frequent airing, this will be damageable to the yeast.

Contextual knowledge thus becomes contextualized knowledge for the solving of a weaker problem. Our contextual knowledge-based system was working with a neural network representation of the wine fermentation step (the deep knowledge).

2.6 "Computer-Mediated Group Work" Project (1997–1999)

Brézillon et al. [14] present the research project "computer-mediated collaborative work" that consisted of the description of the cognitive and contextual aspects involved in a situation of collaborative understanding when two or more subjects interact with each other via a computer network to achieve a joint goal and to understand a new notion. For example, subjects had to co-build an answer to questions like "How does the oyster make pearls?" and "How water becomes mineral?".

Our goal was to identify the nature of the mental models built by the subjects during the understanding of a document and the mechanisms underlying this understanding, knowing that it has been enriched by a preliminary and dynamic phase of collaboration mediated by computer. Several types of cognitive indicators are used: descriptors of verbal interaction during collaboration, analysis of eye movements during reading and error rate to assess comprehension. A mapping of all these indicators provided a global view of the collaborative understanding process. Our contribution was a modeling of the verbal interaction during the collaboration based on contextual graphs.

The collaborative process of answer building started with a first phase of building of the shared context of the question understanding. Each subject introduces a contextual element from his/her individual working context. The other subject may agree or ask for an explanation and eventually negotiates with the first subject. Thus, subjects agree on their shared context satisfying both of them. In a second phase, the subjects organize, assemble and structure the contextual elements of the shared context to generate a proceduralized context that will be integrated in the answer building.

The experiment setup was in two phases: a phase of collaboration initialization and then the reading/comprehension phase by analysis of eye movements and answers to questions. We only discuss the first phase. Subjects followed naturally a dialog model in four phases, namely reformulate the question, find an example, gather domain knowledge and build the answer either by looking for characteristics or by assembling explanation elements (for an integration).

The collaboration model concerned four paths: none of subjects had knowledge about the answer, subjects had some elements of explanation but were not able to build the answer, the two subjects co-built the answer, each bringing elements to share with the other, and when one subject knew the answer, she spent all the allocated time to explain the other subject the elements of the answer (often developing explanation based on her personal contextual knowledge).

Four main observations could be made about the role that context plays in this experiment.

First, subjects can know the answer but not the elements of the answer. As a consequence, they try to exploit their shared context to express an external and superficial viewpoint on a possible answer.

Second, subjects begin by repeating aloud the question to be sure to understand correctly the question (with a possible correction by the other subject), i.e. to be able to activate their mental representations to develop their joint mental model for addressing the question.

Three, subjects can give an answer at different granularities according to the shared context constituted from their respective working contexts and understanding of the question (e.g. say "gas" instead of "CO_2" for sparkling water).

Four, subjects first gather contextual information for establishing the shared context about their understanding of the question and second for building a proceduralized context for the answer. We use in this monograph mainly the modeling of the shared-context building as example of this application.

2.7 A Focus on the Task Realization and not the Task Model

We started our research on context in the engineering domain in which exist formal models of equipment to monitor. Globally, although domain knowledge is accessible such as reports or rules, some external elements have to be considered concerning how to use domain knowledge with respect to the actor, the task the actor must realize, the situation in which the task is realized and the local environment where there are resources available for the task. All these external elements constrain the normal functioning of what is in the focus. Actor, task, situation and environment are sources of contextual knowledge that matters for a focus of attention.

We discovered rapidly that modeling context supposes that actor's focus concerns the realization of the task, not a model of the task. The unique consideration of a task model is insufficient for developing a competent computer software: It is important also to consider the context in which the task is realized by an actor. Actors interpret the task model (e.g. procedures of the company that are considered as mandatory) according to the contextual information collected to determine how to address the focus of attention in the specific context, whatever this way is if policy and strategic decisional levels of the company are respected (e.g. prioritizing a fast solution to avoid a degraded situation in the SEPT project and problems with traveler security and traffic regularity in the SART project). Again, actors use contextual knowledge from sources like the task, the situation and the local environment. As a consequence, context is strongly related to operational knowledge and reasoning, both in models and in the heads of actors. It is the object of Chap. 3.

References

1. Bau, D.Y., Brézillon, P.: Model-based diagnosis of power station control systems: the SEPT experiment. IEEE Expert. **7**, 36–44 (1992)
2. Brézillon, P.: Interpretation and rule packet in expert systems. Application to the SEPT expert system. In: Ramani, S., Chandrasekar, R., Anjaneyulu, K.S.R. (eds.) Knowledge Based Computer Systems. Lecture Notes in Artificial Intelligence, vol. 444, pp. 78–87. Springer Verlag (1990)
3. Brézillon, P., et al.: SART: a system for supporting operators with contextual knowledge. In: Brézillon, P., Cavalcanti, M. (eds.) CONTEXT-97: Modeling and Using Context, pp. 209–222. Rio de Janeiro, Brazil, UFRJ (1997)
4. Brézillon, P., et al.: Representing operational knowledge by contextual graphs. In: Monard, M.C., Sichman, J.S. (eds.) Advances in Artificial Intelligence. Lecture Notes in Artificial Intelligence, vol. 1952, pp. 245–258. Springer, Berlin (2000)
5. Brézillon, P.: Representation of procedures and practices in contextual graphs. Knowl. Eng. Rev. **18**(2), 147–174 (2003)
6. Landauer, C., Bellman, K.: The role of self-referential logics in a software architecture using wrappings. In: ISS'93: Proceedings of 3rd Irvine Software Symposium, pp. 1–12. Irvine. (1993)

7. Pasquier, L., et al.: From representation of operational knowledge to practical decision making in operations. In: Decision Support Through Knowledge Management, pp. 301–320 (2000)
8. Brézillon, P., et al.: Modeling glocal search in a decision-making process. In: PhillipsWren, G., et al. (eds.) DSS 2.0—Supporting Decision Making Process with New Technologies. Frontiers in Artificial Intelligence and Applications, vol. 261, pp. 80–91. IOS Press (2014). https://doi.org/10.3233/978161499399580
9. Kabil, A., et al.: Contextual interface for operator-simulator interaction. In: Christiansen, H., et al. (eds.) CONTEXT-15: Modeling and Using Context, Lecture Notes in Artificial Intelligence, vol. 9405, pp. 483–488. Springer (2015)
10. Hoffman, R.R.: The cognitive psychology of expertise and the domain of interpreting. Interpreting 2(1–2), 189–230 (1997)
11. Brézillon, P.: Contextual modeling of group activity. In: Brézillon, P., et al. (eds.) CONTEXT-17: Modeling and Using Context, Lecture notes in Artificial Intelligence, vol. 10257, pp. 113–126. Springer International Publishing AG, Heldeiberg (2017)
12. Agabra, J., et al.: Contextual knowledge-based system: a study and design in enology. In: Brézillon, P., Cavalcanti, M. (eds.) CONTEXT-97: First International and Interdisciplinary Conference on Modeling and Using Context, pp. 351–362. Rio de Janeiro, Brazil, UFRJ (1997)
13. Laird, J.E., et al.: Soar: an architecture for general intelligence. Artif. Intell. 33(1), 1–64 (1987)
14. Brézillon, P., et al.: Modeling collaborative construction of an answer by contextual graphs. In: Proceedings of IPMU, pp. 11–13. Paris, France (2006)

Chapter 3
Operational Knowledge and Context

The chapter shows that context is intertwined with operational knowledge and reasoning in real-world applications (and more particularly in domains where knowledge occurs in an operational form that is different of knowledge in formal models).

First, we differentiate different types of knowledge according to our goal of context modeling and to the focus that is associated with. We introduce the distinction between contextual knowledge, external knowledge (and the link between them) and the notion of proceduralized context used in association with practice development.

Second, we integrate actors that have this knowledge in their head and concretize their mental representation of the task realization, which makes their knowledge operational and leads to a mental model for a given focus.

The third part discusses the modeling of operational knowledge, and the fourth part the indirect way (a bottom-up approach) to model operational knowledge from experience when a direct modeling of operational knowledge is not possible. The important points of our research in this chapter and the two following ones are called "key points" in the text and are summed up in Table 6.1 and discussed in Chapter 6.

3.1 Contextual Knowledge and External Knowledge

Context is the framework that reveals *know how* [1]. In other words, knowledge is the information that is integrated and understood in the mind of an actor, information resulting from data interpretation. The *focus of attention* of the actor allows differentiating two parts of context, namely contextual knowledge and external knowledge (**key point 1**).

© The Author(s), under exclusive license to Springer Nature Switzerland AG 2023
P. Brézillon, *Research on Modeling and Using Context Over 25 Years*,
SpringerBriefs in Computer Science,
https://doi.org/10.1007/978-3-031-39338-9_3

The main focuses considered in our research concern task realization, decision-making and problem solving that are developed in sequences of steps. The focus moves from one step to the following one, and, at each step, there is a particular context that is related to the focus.

Contextual knowledge constitutes a set of elements more or less related to the focus in a flat way at a given step. *External knowledge* concerns elements that are not important for the focus at the considered step. The frontier between contextual and external knowledge is porous, and elements move between them during the progression of the focus of attention from one step to the following one.

Contextual knowledge is personal to an actor and is evoked by situations and events. It is something that is stored in long-term memory and recalled as a whole in the working memory at some step of the focus. The distinction between contextual knowledge and external knowledge avoids the problem of the infinite dimension of context evoked by McCarthy [2], this infinite dimension being linked to the external knowledge.

As said in the presentation of the TACTIC project (see Sect. 2.4), actors are guided by their mental representations from where they extract a mental model corresponding to the focus of attention at a given step, the situation in which the task is being realized, and the local environment where resources are available. The mental representation of an actor corresponds to the personal context where the actor will extract a mental model. Personal context of the actor is something important about knowledge that is not captured in traditional knowledge measures, such as its operational and dynamical organizations. Moreover, knowledge organization (and thus actors' mental representations of a problem) is different from an actor to another one.

Consider an exercise of mathematics in a college. For reaching the goal of the exercise, the teacher (normally) decomposes the problem in several questions acting as successive steps of students' reasoning (the focus being the problem solving). When the focus step in on question 2, elements used for solving question 1 leave contextual knowledge (for external knowledge), but the answer to question 1 (and new elements) enters contextual knowledge related to the focus on question 2. The selection of the contextual knowledge related to the focus is a kind of first instantiation of the contextual knowledge or background context that needs some specification to perfectly fit the focus step. The precision and differentiation brought to the contextual knowledge (the second instantiation) is obtained by a proceduralization process. *Knowing how* is "instantiating by doing", and contextual knowledge obeys a dynamic of instantiation and proceduralization during action.

This proceduralization converts contextual knowledge into a *proceduralized context*, that is, the part of contextual knowledge used in the focus at the current step (**key point 2**).

The proceduralized context is quite similar, in the spirit at least, to a chunk of knowledge [3, 4] and, in its creation, to Clancey's [5] view of diagnosis as the construction of a situation-specific model. The proceduralized context is built progressively along the focus progression (e.g. practice development). It is activated and structured to satisfy the focus of attention [6].

If contextual knowledge is background knowledge for the focus, the proceduralized context is foreground knowledge, that is, immediately useful at the given step on which the focus is. Thus, it is possible to explain how the proceduralized context was built, the reasons behind choices (contextual elements considered and their instantiations), the alternatives abandoned (actions corresponding to the values of the contextual elements not retained), etc.

3.2 Mental Models[1] of Operational Knowledge

In a real-world application, experts develop their experience as a mental representation of their task realizations (use of domain knowledge in different contexts). Such a mental representation corresponds the *operational knowledge* that the expert mobilizes for addressing the focus of attention, experience relying on operational knowledge as well as domain knowledge.

In the TACTIC project, experts were asked to develop mental maps as a semi-structured expression of their mental models (this was done in another project in medicine too, [7]). Although working on the same domain knowledge, experts' mental maps show depth- and breadth-first strategies for modeling how they address a focus. Usually, reasoning is between a "depth-first" strategy and a "breadth-first" strategy.

The "depth-first" strategy goes to the finest possible granularity of the context on a line of reasoning in order to anticipate as much as possible the course of events from a maximum of instantiated contextual elements. This strategy assumes that we are able to contextualize what we have to do and how to get there quickly. This strategy allows studying the technical feasibility of an approach as well as the needs in terms of resources before, in a second step, gradually expands the approach. The focus of attention is put in context.

Conversely, the "breadth-first" strategy is applied when it is necessary to consider first all possible options (potential lines of reasoning) before choosing a line for making decision. Mental representations in a breadth-first strategy allow experts to keep an "open mind", for example, for detecting weak signals. Such experts reason at a strategic decisional level and do not consider low-level details of contextualization of the focus. Conversely, expert maps made by experts in a depth-first strategy can be used to decide rapidly at the operational decisional level.

The breadth-first strategy is observed in expert maps where the contextual knowledge represented is not limited to the object of the focus of attention. For example, "environment" was considered by an expert in the TACTIC project only as a part of "situation", even if, by itself, environment is an important source of context on

---

[1] We distinguish the expressions "mental representation" and "mental model" used in some disciplines because the two expressions differ, for us, as much as interpolation and extrapolation in mathematics. A mental representation gives a background view on how to address a given focus in different contexts, while a mental model concerns how to address that focus in a specific context.

the battlefield map. The reason is that experts consider environment through what soldiers on the ground really need to know for realizing their task. It is only when there is contact with the enemy that experts zoom in on the exact location of the enemy (e.g. in a city or in landscape). The experts thus are more interested in an external event through its effect on the focus of soldiers rather than by the origin of this event.

The interplay between depth- and breadth-first strategies is considered in the literature under various approaches. The glocal[2] search also is based on a cycle beginning with a phase of fast exploration for finding zones of interest (global search) followed by a phase of fine-grained analysis of the zones judged of interest (local search).

In the FlexMIm project, we pointed out that Anatomical Pathology (AP) physicians follow procedures that include a gross examination (visual examination of organs), dissection and sampling of surgical specimens according to standardized protocols (global search) and then a microscopic examination of stained tissue sections (local search). A lesson learned in this project was that digital slides are analyzed at two levels: global and local.

At the global level, ACPs enter an exploratory phase that is guided by their knowledge (their mental representation of the problem). Global properties of an image allow distinguishing objects and zones of interest in complex scenes for working on them (selection, recognition and control of action).

At the local level, there is a zoom further down to the zone of interest. The grain size at which ACPs choose to zoom (magnification at either $\times 20$ or $\times 40$) affects not only what they can discern but also what become indistinguishable, thus permitting the mind to ignore confusing details.

Moreover, ACPs cannot use tools like pattern recognition because object identification is not binary. Instead, they select and combine features as criteria in favor of the presence, the absence or uncertainty on features (in a kind of "image wall"). ACPs give a value of the feature for evaluating the criterion that depends on ACPs' experience. The modeling of the glocal search is an important process of their reasoning in diagnosis.

Context-aware systems distinguish two types of context: the "local" context (contextual knowledge) that is close of the focus and highly detailed and the "distant" context (external knowledge) that is general. In the spirit of Sowa's [8] conceptual graphs, all the concepts can be expanded in the local context and aggregated in the distant context. Local details are needed for expressing the local interactions with a structure. The global context is needed to tell the actor which other interesting parts of the structure exist and where they are. Global information is important even in the simple interpretation of local details.

---

[2] http://en.wikipedia.org/wiki/Glocal.

3.3 Mental Maps of Operational Knowledge

Two types of reasoning (depth-first strategy and breadth -first strategy) are illustrated in Figs. 3.1 and 3.2, respectively (from the TACTIC project). Only the general shape of the two maps matters for the purpose of this section. The mental representation of the task "Give a reconnoitering order" (find out what the enemy is doing) was elaborated by knowledge acquisition techniques from a panel of ten experts that routinely used the battlefield simulator for different purposes. Each expert expressed in a mind map the knowledge they generally used for realizing the task (the mental representation), and they simplified the corresponding map for the specific scenario proposed (i.e. their mental model in the specific context of the scenario). Gray items in both figures correspond to the contextual elements of the mental representation not used in the mental model developed for the specific scenario on which experts had to work.

Figure 3.1 shows how the operational expert (a developer) organizes his knowledge in depth-first way for analyzing more what the execution of an action on the simulator is than what the action is on the battlefield (i.e. in the simulation).

Figure 3.2 shows the knowledge organization of the tactical expert (a simulator trainer) in a breadth-first way, which is very close to that of the operator interacting

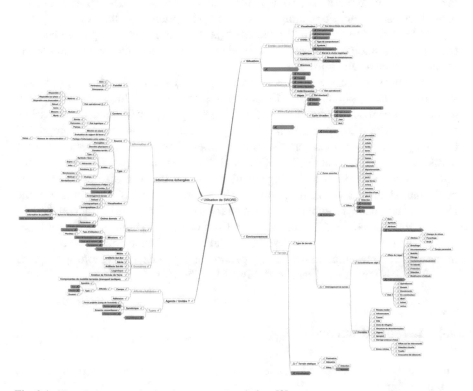

Fig. 3.1 Knowledge organization in an operational view [9]

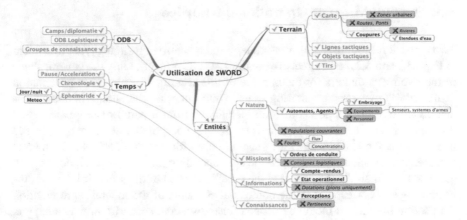

Fig. 3.2 Knowledge organization in a tactical view [9]

with the simulator (the end-user). The focus is on the position of the mission in the context of the battlefield and lets all other problems remain at the periphery of their mental representation. The expert also may introduce links between leaves in the mind map to express his strong compilation of the contextual elements in their mental representation. For example, the item "perceptions" (at the bottom-right in Fig. 3.2) is linked to the item "Ephemeris" (at the middle-left in Fig. 3.2) because the useful information on weather and day/night only addresses the question of the soldier's vision around him.

The comparison of the Figs. 3.1 and 3.2 (F1 and F2 in this paragraph) shows several interesting points. First, F1 is a representation of a local reasoning with a detailed organization (depth of 8 levels) on the ground with specific items like "agent", "situation", "information" exchanged, while F2 represents a more global reasoning with an organization at a general level (depth of 4 levels) with general items like "ground", "entities", "ODB" and "time chronology". F1 and F2 show different contextual knowledge organizations. The difference also appears at the contextual element level with more than 100 elements in F1 (60% retained in the mental model), while F2 contains 38 elements (but 85% retained in the mental model), the consequence being different proceduralized contexts exhibiting different types of reasoning. It appears clearly that the mental model of the tactical expert is close of the mental representation, while the operational expert develops more specialized mental models than mental representations for different scenarios.

3.4 Lessons Learned

There are five lessons learned on operational knowledge and mental representations in this example.

First, tactical experts tend to develop mental representations (as seen on their mental maps) with a predominant parallel structure (breadth-first strategy), while operational experts are more prone to model specific problems by developing detailed mental representations with a predominant series structure (depth-first strategy). Such a detailed mental representation is close to a mental model. Two experts may have different mental representations, but can reach the same conclusion.

Second, the quality of the task realization depends directly on the expert's knowledge about the task realization, the situation and the local environment. The operational expert focuses on the precise understanding of the problem at hand, while a tactical expert seeks a solution for the problem at hand considered among other problems. The main difference between experts' mental representations is the consideration of the methods to employ the contextual knowledge for realizing the task rather than of the consideration of the task model only.

Three, the tactical expert thinks in an organized and structured way, avoids assumptions leading to unrealistic scenarios and identifies actions that can be performed in parallel. The operational expert executes actions sequentially without paying a particular attention to the logic of the task. The latter eventually may add subtasks or change the order of the subtasks, while the tactical expert applies the general scenario (the procedure), first, by collecting contextual information and, second, by selecting the best strategy to apply, with respect to the proceduralized context.

Four, the tactical expert has a holistic view of the task realization and discriminates relevant from useless contextual elements in a kind of "cognitive simulation" to look ahead in the task realization. The operational expert has a context-centered view of the task realization and, thus, reasons reactively (in a pure proceduralization process), discovering the task during its realization, sometimes missing some details, considering irrelevant aspects or establishing no links between the different steps.

Five, expert maps (like shown inn Figs. 3.1 and 3.2) represent actors' working contexts (i.e. their mental representations of the task realization), with contextual elements, their instantiations and their organization. A whole expert map corresponds to a mental representation, the part of the expert map that is not shaded corresponds to the "mental model" used by experts to decision-making during the scenario. The simple observation of such actor maps shows there is not a unique model (and representation) of all the working contexts (see the two expert maps in Figs. 3.1 and 3.2).

3.5 Indirect Modeling from Direct Experience Reuse

The direct reuse of known practices instead of restarting from scratch is observed in domains where experts' experience is preferred to domain where knowledge is weakly (or not) formalized. Experts rely on highly compiled experience, and the reuse of their experience is never direct because it was obtained in numerous specific contexts. Thus, reusing a past experience implies that the actor follows three steps.

- "Contextualization": find a relevant solution of a known past experience related to the experience at hand;
- "Decontextualization": identify the task model of the past experiences (i.e. retrieving the contextual elements from their instantiations);
- "Recontextualization": establish new instantiations for the contextual elements of the model of the past experience in the context at hand.

This process of contextualization-decontextualization–recontextualization (CDR) is used in different domains. For example, Brannen [10] analyzes the two first attempts of the Walt Disney Company made at internationalization: Tokyo Disneyland (1983) and Disneyland Paris (1992). The initial goal was to implant a strict copy of the initial park at Anaheim (USA) in Japan as well as in France, and the internationalization challenge was assessing the fit of what they wish to transfer abroad with the new host environment.

Generally, firms transfer their whole organizations, including business models, steeped in image-based, ideological, people-dependent management that are even more closely related to context and sociocultural environment in which they are enacted. However, if the source is significantly foreign from target, the transferred assets may not fit the target context in the host country. It was the case of Disneyland Paris, the context of the French target was too different (recontextualization was mandatory, as discovered several years later by Walt Disney Company), while the direct transfer to Tokyo Disneyland was a success (no CDR was needed).

Fan et al. [11] applied the CDR process in the search for a scientific workflow (SWF) in virtual screening of the H5N1 virus (see Fig. 3.3): A researcher extracts a successful SWF from a repository that is considered close of the focus (phase of

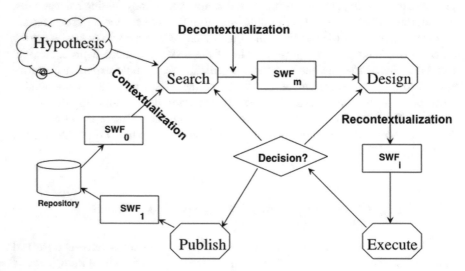

Fig. 3.3 CDR approach in workflow life cycle (from [11])

contextualization), extracts the corresponding SWF model (phase of decontextualization) and, finally, instantiates differently the SWF model in the working context (phase of recontextualization). Then, a workflow engine ensures the execution phase in which input data are consumed according to the instantiated SWF and output data are produced as results. If it is a success, the new scientific workflow is put in the repository for other scientists. Otherwise, a new iteration is needed by reconsidering either the phase of decontextualization for finding a new model or by trying a different recontextualization of a new scientific workflow.

The experience acquired by the researcher during this process relies on context management. This modeling allows making context, and consequently operators' behavior, explicit.

References

1. Brézillon, P., Pomerol, J.-C.: Is context a kind of collective tacit knowledge? In: Jacovi, M., Ribak, A. (eds.) European CSCW 2001 Workshop on Managing Tacit Knowledge, pp. 23–29. Bonn, Germany (2001)
2. McCarthy, J.: Notes on formalizing context. In: International Joint Conference on Artificial Intelligence, pp. 555–560 (1993)
3. Miller, G.A.: The magic number seven plus or minus two: some limits on our capacity for processing information. Psychol. Rev. **63**, 91–97 (1956)
4. Schank, R.C.: Dynamic Memory, A Theory of Learning in Computers and People. Cambridge University Press (1982)
5. Clancey, W.J.: Simulating activities: relating motives, deliberation, and attentive coordination. Cogn. Syst. Res. **3**(3), 471–499 (2002)
6. Pomerol, J.-C., Brézillon, P.: Dynamics between contextual knowledge and proceduralized context. In: Bouquet, P., et al. (eds.) CONTEXT-99: Modeling and Using Context. Lecture Notes in Artificial Intelligence, vol. 1688, pp. 284–295. Springer Verlag (1999)
7. Brézillon, P., et al.: Modeling glocal search in a decision-making process. In: PhillipsWren, G., et al. (eds.) DSS 2.0—Supporting Decision Making Process with New Technologies. Frontiers in Artificial Intelligence and Applications, vol. 261, pp. 80–91. IOS Press (2014). https://doi.org/10.3233/978161499399580
8. Sowa, J.F.: Knowledge Representation: Logical, Philosophical, and Computational Foundations. Brooks Cole Publishing Co, Pacific Grove, CA (2000)
9. Brézillon, P.: CxG-based simulation of group activity. In: ISTE OpenScience. ISTE Ltd., London, openscience.fr, vol. 2-1 (2018). https://doi.org/10.21494/ISTE.OP.2018.0231
10. Brannen, M.Y.: When Mickey loses face: recontextualization, semantic fit, and the semiotics of foreignness. Acad. Manag. Rev. **29**(4), 593–616 (2004)
11. Fan, X., et al.: A context-based framework for improving decision making in scientific workflow. In: ICCRD-2011: Proceedings of the 3rd International Conference on Computer Research and Development, Shanghai, China (2011)

Chapter 4
From Context Modeling
to Implementation for Individuals

This chapter presents the main points of an effective pragmatic approach on context for the modeling of context for its use by an actor in real-world applications, from the conceptual aspects (like the concept of contextual element), the operational aspects discussed in the specific domain of task realization (with the differences between the procedures of the company and the practices developed by actors on the ground) and the context-based formalism of representation leading to the implementation called contextual graphs (CxG) for the focus of one actor. The chapter ends, by a kind of reverse engineering, on the assimilation of contextual graphs to a base of experiences based on the task realization modeled. As for the previous chapter and the following one, different key points of our research are identified in this chapter.

4.1 Conceptual Aspects of Context

Brézillon and Pomerol [1] defined context as "what constrains the focus without intervening in it explicitly". In our applications, the focuses that we considered in our applications were on decision-making, problem solving and task realization. The definition implies that one cannot speak of context in an abstract way (**key point 3**). Context and focus are interdependent, the context makes focus explicit, and focus of attention defines the relevant contextual elements at each step.

As a consequence, the means to implement the focus are as important as the focus itself (**key point 4**).

The organization of the contextual knowledge, which gives the structure of actor's mental representation, depends on the experience of the actor that realizes the task. These observations lead to the conclusion that, at the operational level, context is fed by four sources of *contextual elements*, namely the actor, the focus, the situation and the environment (**key point 5**).

P. Brézillon, *Research on Modeling and Using Context Over 25 Years*,
SpringerBriefs in Computer Science,
https://doi.org/10.1007/978-3-031-39338-9_4

Another conclusion is that, conversely to other representation formalisms, it is important to distinguish the contextual element and its instantiation (**key point 6**).

The explicit introduction of contextual elements for representing contextual knowledge and the distinction with their values offer new perspectives: The acquisition of a new practice corresponds to the addition of either a new contextual element (learning by accommodation) or a new value for an existing contextual element (learning by assimilation), the latter case leading to simply a refinement of the practice. The type of values can be either qualitative or quantitative. For example, the contextual element "Temperature?" may have qualitative values like "warm" or "cold", but, according to the focus, quantitative values like "24.5 °C" are possible instead of "warm".

A qualitative instantiation of a contextual element can be another contextual element (see examples, in [2]). During focus progress, the instantiation of contextual elements may be altered by either an external or an internal event. The external event corresponds to an unpredicted event (e.g. the power supply being cut off) and thus is not represented in the task realization. An internal event occurs as the result of an action execution. For example, a fuse becomes too hot and blows. The change of instantiation of a contextual element modifies the working context. It may lead either to a change of task to realize if the initial hypothesis is abandoned for the development of a practice for another task realization or to modify the conclusion of the task realization.

The association of conceptual and operational views, which ensures a direct implementation of the conceptual model of context, is obtained thanks to the introduction of the notion of *contextual element* that allows to bridge the two views. Figure 4.1 synthetizes our approach up to now from the conceptual view to the operational view. This double viewpoint (conceptual and operational frameworks) constitutes the ground of all our (successful) research in real-world applications.

The notions of contextual knowledge and proceduralized context being introduced in Sect. 3.1, we now discuss on the working context. The working context (i.e. the mental representation evoked previously) contains the contextual elements that an actor associates with a focus, all the known values of each contextual element and the chosen instantiation. Arriving at a contextual element, its instantiation is necessary for the focus progress and leads to a proceduralization of part of the working context (the proceduralized context evoked previously) and the action to execute (see also [3]). The instantiations can be known prior to the task realization either provided by the actor when (and if) needed or found by a system in the local environment.

The organization of the contextual elements can be illustrated by the onion metaphor that has been proposed in the SART project and also used in the application concerning wine fermentation (see Sect. 2.5). The focus (step by step) is the onion heart, and contextual elements can be organized in layers around the heart. Figure 4.2 illustrates the solving of the incident "Sick traveler in a train" in the SART project (see Sect. 4.2). The step "Stop at the next station" (the focus step) is the onion heart, and dotted lines around it represent the successive layers of contextual elements. For instance, the contextual element "Procedures" is in the first layer, "Past experience" in the second one, which is an explanation for using procedure, etc.

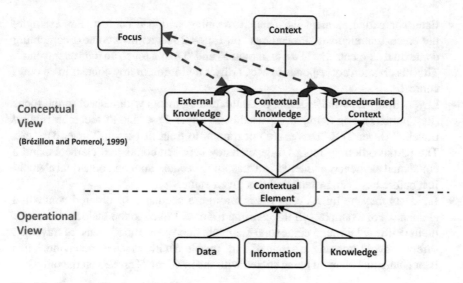

Fig. 4.1 Conceptual and operational views on contextual elements

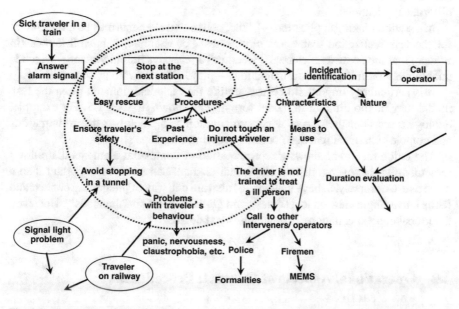

Fig. 4.2 Contextual organization in the incident "Ill traveler in a train" (SART project)

There are several interesting points for our modeling of context for real-world applications with the onion metaphor:

- A focus step has a meaning within a context, even if contextual knowledge does not intervene explicitly at this step.

- Each contextual element itself has a meaning within a context. For example, the contextual element "Procedures" on Fig. 4.2 has its own context containing contextual elements like "Past experience" and "Do not touch an injured traveler". This observation corresponds to McCarthy's definition of any context in an outer context.
- Layers imply a partial ordering of contextual elements with respect to the focus (**key point 7**). For example, "Procedures" (layer 1) < "Don't touch an injured traveler" (layer 2) < "Driver are not trained to treat ill persons" layer 3) < etc. The partial ordering implies a dependency between contextual elements, and a contextual element is of interest in a reasoning because another contextual element just before has been instantiated to a given value.
- Incidents may be linked each other through a sequence of ordered contextual elements. For example, "Ill traveler in a train" is linked to the incident "Traveler on the railway" through contextual elements like "procedure", "ensure traveler's safety", "avoid stopping in a tunnel" and "problem with traveler's behaviors"; this later contextual element being shared with the incident "Traveler on the railway".

The onion metaphor allows the development of explanations of different natures and at different levels of detail corresponding to the layers. It is useful in many different applications.

In the wine-making application [4], "far" contextual elements may be more crucial for the task realization than some close ones. For example, it is well-known (in France) that the contextual element "weather" a few days before vintage—which is qualitatively far from "wine fermentation"—plays a central role in wine-making.

It is particularly important because, unlike the technical domain, often the task model may be too difficult to model formally as shown in Sect. 1.5. For example, enologists consider the step of wine fermentation as a black box due to numerous and complex chemical reactions occurring during this step.

The onion metaphor shows a representation of contextual elements that allows remembering that even a distant contextual element can be more important than a close one. Conversely, fisheye views [5, 6] also are one way of integrating context and focus into a single view on local details and global context simultaneously. However, the global context cannot be exploited as local details.

4.2 Operational Aspects of Context: Procedures and Practices

Formally, a practical unit of reasoning can be expressed as "IF P1, P2, ... THEN C1". In a logical and theoretical reasoning (e.g. a procedure), the action leads to the conclusion C1 that is added alone to the knowledge base. In a practical reasoning (e.g. a practice), the premises P1, P2, ... stay attached to the conclusion; that is, C1 has a meaning coming from the premises. An element like C1 is defined in a context of use (P1, P2, … are true), context that is lost in procedures applicable to a large class of similar problems.

A *practice* is a contextualization of the procedure in a particular context (**key point 8**). Such a practice generally is the "best practice" in that specific context, and there are as many best practices as encountered contexts.

Concretely, a task model often is built from a decontextualization process of a large set of practices to extract what is common to a maximum of practices. In the SART project, procedures are established in a kind of CDR process by analyzing incident-solving reports (identification of the contextualization in the practices) that are formalized (decontextualization) by merging all reports on a given incident in a procedure supposed to be applicable to the largest class possible of incident solving. Train drivers recontextualize procedures when needed because procedures are exceptionally applicable directly to "real-world" incidents. In their daily work, actors have to apply the procedure in specific contexts that require its adaptation (i.e. recontextualization).

As a consequence, actors use their operational knowledge and experience (their mental representation of the focus) to develop practices that (re)contextualize the procedure during their task realization in the specific context.

If a procedure is a representation of a task model, modeling practices, which are developed by actors on the basis of a procedure, lead to as many practices as contexts in which the task model is applied. Generally, practices differ each other by few elements; thus, it is possible to give a unique global representation to all practices for a given focus [7].

The CxG representation formalism (presented in the next section) allows a unified modeling of all the practices developed by actors in a unique contextual graph. In comparison with the task model, the contextual graph represents a *contextualized task model* where all the paths correspond to intertwined practices developed by actors for representing the procedure in different contexts (**key point 9**).

In the CxG formalism, practices are paths from the input to the output of a contextual graph, and often a practice differs from other practices (i.e. other paths) generally on small parts at the level of contextual elements, for example, by different instantiations of a contextual element.

The contextualized task model and practices are at the tactical decisional level, while the development of a specific practice and the corresponding proceduralized context building are at the operational decisional level (**key point 10**) (see [2, 8], for an application concerning the self-training of car drivers).

4.3 Implementation as Contextual Graphs (CxG_1.0 Version)

The first version of the contextual graphs, called CxG_1.0, was the object of the Pasquier's Ph.D. dissertation [9]. The dissertation presents the history of the elaboration of the CxG formalism since the first ruleset developed in the SART project. Other references covering this work are Brézillon et al. [10, 11] and a recent synthesis including the CxG extension for group activity can be found in Brézillon [12], where activity is taken in the sense of "task-centered activity". Since 2002, the CxG software has been corrected, adapted, enriched by a number of students that I want to warmly thank.

The operational definition of context and the study in depth of different aspects of context have allowed the design and implementation of the context-based representation formalism called contextual graphs (CxG). The CxG formalism has been used with success in all the applications cited in the Sect. 4.1 (except the SEPT application).

We limit our purpose in this book to the main features of the formalism and software needed to understand the lessons learned about context and its role in applications.

If the conceptual and operational frameworks allowed to implement and use the CxG formalism, reciprocally, findings made at the CxG formalism level led to reinforce the conceptual modeling of context. For example, a contextual element is modeled in the CxG formalism as a pair {contextual node, recombination node} that define branches with different instantiations of the contextual element corresponding to different actions that can take place, generating different practices (**key point 11**).

Formally, a contextual graph is a directed acyclic series–parallel graph with exactly one root and one exit because operators have only one goal and branches express only different strategies, depending on the context, to achieve this goal (**key point 12**).

Figure 4.3 shows how a task realization is modeled under the form of a contextual graph in the CxG software. Actions are green square boxes.

Contextual elements are represented by a contextual node (blue circle with a number) and a recombination node (blue circle without number) where end the two exclusive paths coming from the contextual nodes.

Activities (contextual subgraphs identified by actors as independent of the main graph) are represented by pink elongated ovals.

An Executive Structure of Independent Activities (ESIA) is represented by two vertical red bars with independent activities between them. These independent activities (i.e. a decision made on one branch of the ESIA does not influence decision-making on other branches) can be treated in any order (or in parallel), but all must be executed before to resume the traversal of the main graph.

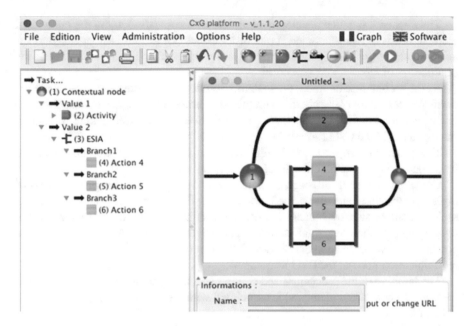

Fig. 4.3 Four elements of a contextual graph

An example of use of an ESIA in the FlexMIm project is a voting system for criteria appraisal. The twelve customizable criteria were put on twelve branches of an ESIA, that is, accessible in any order and weighting of criteria (and some of them can be left on the side by some actors). The evaluation of the criteria is obtained directly by observation or may require an additional analysis.

For example, a criterion concerning "pseudo-stratification or nuclear pseudo-stratification" needs the contextual information "presence" or "absence" of pseudo-stratification. Then, this result is used to modify the contextual element "vote" that may be incremented (vote = vote + 1) in an action if the expert judges that the criterion are verified.

Finally, once all the branches of the ESIA are checked, the final value of the contextual element "vote" is used to make the decision after the ESIA.

From key point 5, contextual elements come from four heterogeneous sources (actor, focus, situation and environment). A contextual node corresponds to a question (e.g. "Temperature?"), the different known values (e.g. "cold", "warm", "hot") correspond to different possible actions to execute in the specific context (e.g. "take a T shirt" for "warm"), and the selection of one these values (the instantiation of the contextual element in the context at hand) will lead to the execution of the action. Between the contextual and recombination nodes, there are as many exclusive branches as known practices.

Thus, when a practice development arrives at a contextual node, the contextual element needs to be instantiated at one of its values (known initially or asked to the actor) to select the corresponding branch and progresses in the development of the practice.

At the recombination node, the instantiation does not matter anymore, since the corresponding action (and not those on the other branches of the contextual element) has been completed. This modeling of contextual elements offers a kind of context management in the CxG formalism.

The proceduralized context is the sequence of contextual elements that are instantiated during the practice development (**key point 13**).

Contextual elements are organized in a contextual graph in the spirit of "nest of dolls" (matriochka) and always defined (embedded) with respect to another contextual element as said by McCarthy [13]. As a consequence, there is never partial overlapping of the contextual elements and any contextual element is itself in a context, that is, inside another contextual element (between a contextual node and a recombination node in the CxG formalism).

The building of the proceduralized context (i.e. the generation of the sequence of instantiated contextual elements) is associated with the development of the practice (**key point 14**).

Contextual elements provide a structure to the contextualized task model at the tactical level, and the instantiation process, associated with the practice development, is at the operational level (**key point 15**).

Series–parallel graphs are used in the literature in a wide range of applications, the most common being electrical circuits [14] and scheduling problems [15]. In these domains, flows follow all the branches simultaneously while in a contextual graph only one path at a time is followed because only one instantiation can be activated at a time for a contextual element.

Moreover, each path in a graph (from the input to the output) corresponds to a unique practice developed for a given focus. As presented in Sect. 3.3, a contextual graph has a parallel structure for the tactical expert who wants to "keep an open mind" and has a series structure for the operational expert who prefers to focus on the details of the task realization at hand without a holistic view.

The syntax of the CxG software is defined in Fig. 4.3 for all the figures representing a contextual graph [16].

The software is written in Java under GNU license, and the contextual graphs developed are written in XML for a reuse in other applications [17]. It is an interface used by actors wishing to edit a contextual graph, reading practices for selecting the best one in his working context, browsing alternatives of a practice, exploring a contextual graph at a different granularity and analyzing contextual information attached to each item (date of creation, comments, etc.).

The mechanisms of aggregation and expansion of activities (at a semantic level) allow actors to observe on one part of the contextual graph or another one according to their focuses of attention, but also with the possibility to hide some parts of the graph (at the syntax level in the same spirit of the aggregation and expansion mechanisms of conceptual graphs, [18]). The actor can define subgraph (i.e. activity) in a contextual graph, and the system then offers the possibility to aggregate it in a node in the contextual graph.

For example, an activity for the operator responsible of the subway line such as "Make your train empty of travelers" is a simple action (the activity), while it is a complex procedure for the train driver (the subgraph in the activity).

All the characteristics of the CxG software thus make possible to study parts of a reasoning and all the variants (the practices). This is particularly interesting to understand variants between two practices, the role plays by a contextual element in the choice of an action instead of another, etc.

All the successive evolutions of the software integrate the functionalities of previous versions. Design and development of the software is user-centered for an intuitive use by non-specialists in computer science and mathematics. Interesting functions of the software are the possibility to link an item to an external document (Word, PDF, web page, etc.), to run an external software, to have the trace of the practice development as a roadmap for an employee, etc. (This was used in a medical application for the modeling of a workflow for sample management in an oncology department, [19].)

The functioning of the platform itself and the management of items can be described themselves in a contextual graph and used in context-based intelligent assistant systems for controlling their activities [20]. An activity—being itself a contextual graph—is stored as an independent XML file and thus can be reused by other software.

4.4 Contextual Graphs as Experience Bases

In our applications, actors were experts in their domain and focused on task realization, decision-making and problem solving. Described in the CxG formalism, these focuses are addressed by contextualized task models (i.e. a contextual graph). As a model of all the known practices developed in different contexts for a given focus, a contextualized task model expresses a kind of local *experience base* [21] associated more with the focus progress than on the focus itself (**Key point 16**). At the difference of previous knowledge bases built from procedures (or equivalent), an experience base concerns the use of practices in different contexts. An intelligent assistant system can reason and accompany an actor on the basis of such experience bases.

In the SART project, we gave the example of the incident-solving "Ill traveler in a train" and underline that this incident solving was connected to the incident-solving "Traveler on the railway" by the network of contextual elements (see Fig. 4.2 in Sect. 4.1). A consequence is the possible sharing of some activities among different focuses of attention in the same domain. More globally, this theme opens a window on research on the grouping of contextual graphs (experience bases) associated with focuses of attention in a given domain and may favor context-based intelligent assistant systems able to tackle several focuses and learn lessons from a holistic integrated view on the domain.

A system using "experience bases" is able to explain, shows alternatives, anticipates by simulation, completes incrementally its experience base by the refinement of existing practices when failing and alerts about the variants abandoned for the practice. The number of practices can be very large, but new practices are learned by the system with the new contexts where they are encountered.

The capabilities of incremental knowledge acquisition, practice learning and explanation allow a system exploiting experience bases to become increasingly "intelligent" because it can benefit of the situation to incrementally acquire new knowledge and learn new practices when it fails. In that sense, the new generation of AI systems to develop is context-based intelligent assistant systems working on local base of experiences corresponding to the realization of different tasks.

Moreover, an experience base developed for a focus can be used by humans for training future experts how to behave in the different ways to make decision according to the variants of the working context [22]. Storing "bad" practices in an experience base also can be an important asset in training and self-training (see an example for car driving in [2]).

We distinguish intelligent systems from intelligent assistant systems. "Intelligent systems" is a term used in formal approaches where, if the knowledge of experts is in the machine, humans do not participate in the task realization (or decision-making, problem solving).

There are two types of learning, either the actor learns from the system or the system learns from the actor. In the former situation, mechanisms like explanation, generation and simulation, the system plays the role of a trainer for novices not familiar with practices developed by other actors. During this learning by the actor, the experience base is exploited in a kind of practice-based learning. The second type of learning occurs when the actor stops the system for specifying a new practice that does not exist in the experience base. Thus, the system plays the role of a learner that will have to modify its experience base.

In the CxG formalism, such a variant occurs generally when a contextual element was not considered up to now (e.g. it kept the same value during all the focus progress), but in that specific context, the instantiation is different and the actor decides to execute a different action. The system thus will enrich incrementally the experience base in a kind of learning.

References

1. Brézillon, P., Pomerol, J.-C.: Contextual knowledge sharing and cooperation in intelligent assistant systems. Le Travail Humain **62**(3), 223–246 (1999)
2. Brézillon, P., Brézillon, J.: Contextualized task modeling. Revue d'Intelligence Artificielle **22**(5), 531–548 (2008)

3. Grimshaw, D.J., Mott, P.L.: Roberts, S.A.: The Role of Context in Decision Making: Some Implications for Database Design. European J. of Inf. System **5**(4), 113–122 (1997)
4. Agabra, J., et al.: Contextual knowledge-based system: a study and design in enology. In: Brézillon, P., Cavalcanti, M. (eds.) CONTEXT-97: First International and Interdisciplinary Conference on Modeling and Using Context, pp. 351–362. UFRJ, Rio de Janeiro, Brazil (1997)
5. Furnas, G.W.: Generalized fisheye views. In: CHI'86: Proceedings of Human Factors in Computing Systems Conference, pp. 16–23 (1986)
6. Pook, S., et al.: Context and interaction in Zoomable user interfaces. In: AVI 2000 Conference Proceedings, pp. 227–231. ACM Press (2000)
7. Brézillon, P.: Task-realization models in Contextual Graphs. In: Dey, A., et al. (eds.) CONTEXT-05: Modeling and Using Context. Lecture Notes in Computer Science, vol, 3554, pp. 55–68. Springer Verlag (2005)
8. Brézillon, J., et al.: Improving driver's situation awareness. In: Kokinov, B., et al. (eds.) CONTEXT-07: Modeling and Using Context, Lecture Notes in Artificial Intelligence, vol. 4635, pp. 136–149. Springer Verlag (2007)
9. Pasquier, L.: Modélisation de raisonnement tenus en contexte. Application à la gestion d'incidents sur une ligne de métro. Thèse de l'Université Paris 6, France, juillet 2002 (2002)
10. Brézillon, P., et al.: SART: a system for supporting operators with contextual knowledge. In: Brézillon, P., Cavalcanti, M. (eds.) CONTEXT-97: Modeling and Using Context, pp. 209–222. UFRJ, Rio de Janeiro (1997)
11. Brézillon, P., et al.: Representing operational knowledge by contextual graphs. In: Monard, M.C., Sichman, J.S. (eds.) Advances in Artificial Intelligence. Lecture Notes in Artificial Intelligence, vol. 1952, pp. 245–258. Springer, Berlin (2000)
12. Brézillon, P.: CxG-Based Simulation of Group Activity, vol. 2-1. In: ISTE OpenScience. ISTE Ltd., London, openscience.fr (2018). https://doi.org/10.21494/ISTE.OP.2018.0231
13. McCarthy, J.: Notes on formalizing context. In: International Joint Conference on Artificial Intelligence pp. 555–560 (1993)
14. Eppstein, D.: Parallel recognition of series-parallel graphs. Inf. Comput. **98**(1), 41–55 (1992)
15. Finta, L., et al.: Scheduling UET–UCT series-parallel graphs on two processors. Theor. Comput. Sci. **162**(2), 323–346 (1996)
16. Brézillon, P.: Representation of procedures and practices in contextual graphs. Knowl. Eng. Rev. **18**(2), 147–174 (2003)
17. Brézillon, P.: Contextualization of scientific workflows. In: Beigl, M., et al. (eds.) CONTEXT-11: Modeling and Using Context, Lecture Notes in Artificial Intelligence, vol. 6967, pp. 40–53. Springer-Verlag (2011)
18. Sowa, J.F.: Knowledge Representation: Logical, Philosophical, and Computational Foundations. Brooks Cole Publishing Co, Pacific Grove, CA (2000)
19. Attieh, E., et al.: Context-based modeling of an anatomo-cyto-pathology. Department Workflow for Quality Control. In: Brézillon, P., et al. (eds.) CONTEXT-13: Modeling and Using Context. Lecture Notes in Artificial Intelligence, vol. 8175, pp. 235–247. Springer, Heidelberg (2013)
20. Brézillon, P.: Chap. 07: context-centered tools for intelligent assistant systems. In: Brézillon, P., Gonzalez, A. (eds.) Context in Computing: A Cross-Disciplinary Approach for Modeling the Real World Through Contextual Reasoning, pp. 97–110. Springer, NY (2014)
21. Brézillon, P.: Context-based development of experience bases. In: Brézillon, P., et al. (eds.) CONTEXT-13: Modeling and Using Context. Lecture Notes in Artificial Intelligence, vol. 8175, pp. 87–100. Springer, Heidelberg (2013)
22. Tahir, H., Brézillon, P.: Contextual graphs platform as a basis for designing a context-based intelligent assistant system. In: Brézillon, P., et al. (eds.) CONTEXT-13: Modeling and Using Context. Lecture Notes in Artificial Intelligence, vol. 8175, pp. 259–273. Springer, Heidelberg (2013)

Chapter 5
From Context Modeling
to Implementation for Group Activity

Our research was initially led for modeling context when the focus is addressed by a unique actor. This section presents the natural extension that includes the management of group members addressing the focus. From the point of view of modeling, implementation and use of context, the changes were an accommodation of the conceptual and operational aspects of context and of the CxG representation formalism.

The accommodation concerns the introduction of a shared context between the working contexts of the group members and the proceduralized context. Other accommodations include different aspects of context and of the CxG simulation in the CxG_2.0 version of the context-based representation formalism. An interesting side effect was to be able to apply the extended version to one actor with the benefits of, on the one hand, a new modeling of the task realization for one actor like for N actors with the notion of independent elementary task and, on the other hand, the CxG simulation tool for expressing task realization "one-shot" but possibly with intermediate variants like the checking of alternatives.

5.1 Conceptual Aspects of Context: The Shared Context

This section presents our view on the shared context (especially its building) based on our experience, first, as one partner in a large project with more than fifteen partners from 6 to 7 different domains (thus participating to the building of the shared context) and, second, as observer in an experiment for modeling verbal exchanges between two actors for collaboratively generating answers to questions [1].

The *shared context* is an extension of the working context of an actor for a task realized by a group of actors. The shared context is elaborated from elements of the individual working contexts of the group members. It evolves continuously according

© The Author(s), under exclusive license to Springer Nature Switzerland AG 2023   41
P. Brézillon, *Research on Modeling and Using Context Over 25 Years*,
SpringerBriefs in Computer Science,
https://doi.org/10.1007/978-3-031-39338-9_5

to interaction among group actors, the group focus and the additions of contextual elements by group members. Shared-context building is the first step of a task realization by a group (**key point 17**).

The group members first gather a maximum of contextual elements without looking for a global picture (in a kind of brainstorming), a member proposes a contextual element supposed to be relevant, and other members accept it or ask for explanation. They accept a new contextual element if they can integrate it in their individual working contexts.

The phase of shared-context building does not concern only contextual knowledge but also external knowledge that the proposal originator can express (e.g. "I had the opportunity to visit a place concerned with this topic a couple of years ago"). Thus, the joint development of the shared context allows group members to keep their mental representations compatible and adjusted to the joint focus [2].

When group members reach a consensus on the content of the shared context, they enter the second phase of the process by organizing, assembling and structuring the instantiated contextual elements of their shared context in a proceduralized context for reaching the group focus at hand.

In the SART project, we observed that operators of subway lines leaving and entering the control room build a temporary shared context for "transferring what's happened" during the last 8 h.

Figure 5.1 illustrates the building of the proceduralized context from group members working contexts and shared context. Actor_1 introduces the contextual element CE_1 from his working context into the shared context. Because CE_1 belongs to Actor_2's working context too, the contextual element is accepted. When Actor_1 proposes the introduction of CE_2, Actor_2, which has no reference to it in his working context, needs explanations for accepting CE_2, and both agree on CE'_2 (compatible interpretation of CE_2 in the shared context). For accepting CE'_2, the receiver builds an interpretation CE"_2 in his working context. Once Actor_2 agrees to the contextual element, the contextual elements of the shared context are combined into a proceduralized context for addressing the focus.

We observed a similar situation in an experiment for modeling verbal exchanges between two actors for collaborative generation of answers to questions like "How does the oyster make pearls?" and "How does water become mineral?" ([1], and Sect. 2.6). The collaborative process of answer building includes a first phase of building of the shared context of the collaboration. Each actor proposes elements from their working context. The other actor may agree or ask for an explanation and eventually negotiate with the first actor.

Finally, actors agree on a shared context satisfying both of them. In the second phase of exploitation of the shared context, the actors organize, assemble and structure the contextual elements of the shared context to generate their proceduralized context that will be integrated in the answer building.

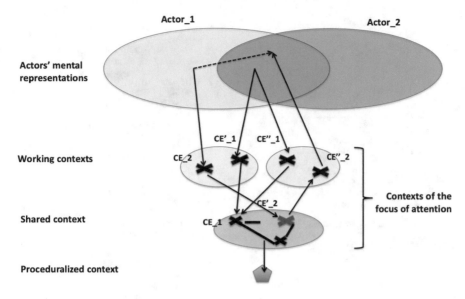

Fig. 5.1 Collaborative building of a proceduralized context

Some results of the "Computer-mediated collaborative work" project are the following. Eleven pairs of participants had to address 16 questions (176 MP3 files of 1min30 correspond to answers). The experiment setup was in two phases: a phase of collaboration (1min30) and then a phase of reading/comprehension phase, including analysis of eye movements and answers to questions.

Here, we only discuss the first phase. Participants followed a process in four steps, namely reformulate the question for reinforcing their understanding, find an example for validating their understanding, gather domain knowledge and elements of their working context and build the answer either by looking for characteristics or by assembling explanation elements (for an integration).

Figure 5.2 represents in the CxG formalism the four types of the collaboration model found.

Three main observations were made from the elicitation phase:

- Subjects had a problem for finding the right granularity of their answer, but gathering contextual information helps to determine the right granularity. When subjects cannot identify the right level of answer granularity, they enter into a process of explanation to justify their proceduralized context.
- Subjects often immediately repeat the question to be sure they understand correctly it and to look for some relationships between elements of the questions and elements of answer from their personal working contexts.
- Subjects can know globally the answer without knowing elements of the answer. As a consequence, subjects express an external and superficial viewpoint. They provide explanations spontaneously to: (1) strengthen a known answer; (2) make progress in the co-construction of the answer; and (3) be sure of the granularity

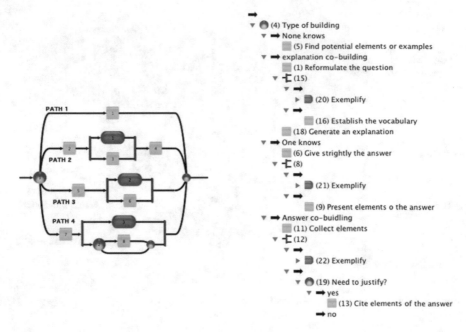

Fig. 5.2 Contextual graph of the identified collaborative answer building processes

of the answer. The explanation is generally less precise than the answer (i.e. at a too general level), but useful between them to reinforce their ties. Several groups of subjects were confused and explained instead of giving the answer (thus with additional details not necessary).

Once the focus is addressed (contextual elements are selected and instantiated), the subjects built the proceduralized context of the answer which enters the actors' mental representation. Later, this proceduralized context may be recalled as a unit for another task realization. Thus, the more an actor experiments, the more the actor acquires structured knowledge, and the more actors work together, the more they reinforce their ties too.

5.2   Operational Aspects of Context: Group Activity

Actors use knowledge and experience to contextualizing a procedure for addressing a focus. It is an activity from an external viewpoint that covers the actor, the focus, the contextual information considered by actors and the various choices made by them to reach the goal. The notion of "activity" extends the notion of "task realization" by including its implementation in a specific context (i.e. the practice development). The task is what an actor must do, and the activity is the (physical and mental) behavior that the actor exhibits during task realization [3].

The notion of activity is particularly adapted to a collective viewpoint on task realization. In collaborative work, several actors work together as group members. This requires an external viewpoint for "sharing out" the task realization between group members. The group activity is related to the way in which the group as a whole realizes the task.

Benitez-Guerrero et al. [4] present the development of an activity (called effective activity) as an instance of an activity model that describes the group members that can participate in the activity, how the activity can be carried out, the family of objects that can be manipulated or produced and which roles group members and objects will play in the activity (what we call the context of the activity).

Their activity model is like a frame to instantiate for any instance of the activity model. In our view, a mental model is also an instance of the mental representation, but the mental representation is not an "activity model" but a unified representation of all the known mental models which are instantiated.

A group activity is more than the simple sum of actor activities because individual activities are interdependent. Each group member generally intervenes at different moments during the development of the group practice, and thus their interventions are independent of each other. Each intervention can be represented as an *independent elementary task* (**key point 18**).

The interaction between actors during the development of the group activity can be understood as the execution of a sequence of independent subtasks in a cyclic use of the contextual graph, the independent elementary tasks being taken in the activities of the group members (**key point 19**).

These changes needed a simple extension of the CxG formalism for the transposition of the task realization by an actor into the realization of a sequence of elementary subtasks realization by different actors.

5.3   The Contextual Graphs Simulation (CxG_2.0 Version)

The extension of the CxG formalism includes, first, the management of several actors and, second, the use of a directed acyclic series–parallel graph to describe the development of the group activity as a sequence of subactivities realized by group members.

This supposes the management of the shared context with the addition of particular contextual elements for modeling the management, on the one hand, of group members' interaction (turn, acceptance, etc.) during group activity development and, on the other hand, of the management of each member's elementary subtasks, which are intertwined in the group activity [5].

The shared context becomes a crucial place for interaction management as well as elementary subtask management in each actor's activity. When a subtask is realized, the shared context is analyzed at the end of the turn to determine which actor must intervene next and which independent subtask that actor must realize [6].

A turn is the traversal of the contextual graph for accomplishing a subtask of a group member and managing the shared context for the next turn (**key point 20**). We obtain a sequence of turns that is generated during the realization of the group activity.

The shared context is composed of the contextual elements of the group activity realization, the contextual elements specific to group management, information transfer between members' activities and interaction management of members during the group activity development.

The shared context plays a more important role than the working context because the shared context is built collectively to realize the group activity. In the CxG_2.0 version, it is the shared context that is attached to the group focus, not individual working contexts.

A simulation corresponds to a sequence of turns (i.e. successive traversals of the contextual graph for a sequential realization of subtasks). The management of the turn sequence is obtained by changes made in the shared context during the previous turn, by the execution of the actions in the subtask and by the instantiation of some "particular" contextual elements [7].

These *reserved contextual elements* define (1) the actor (reserved contextual element SENDER) who was the previous manager, (2) the actor responsible for the subtask in progress (reserved contextual element MANAGER of the turn) and (3) the next manager (reserved contextual element RECIPIENT) and the subtask it has to realize (reserved contextual element TASK_GOAL).

The simulation of a sequence of turns requires a cyclic use of the contextual graph as long as the shared context is modified during the turn (**key point 21**). Such simulations are called *CxG simulations*.

The group management (members and elementary subtasks) is represented in the CxG formalism by a general structure called a *contextual meta-graph*. Figure 5.3, which is obtained from the CxG software, shows the organization of the contextual meta-graph in two windows. The window on the right is the graphical representation of the meta-graph with four contextual elements (blue circles, the contextual nodes with a number and the combination nodes without number) and six activities (pink ovals containing a contextual subgraph where each branch corresponds to an independent subtask). The window on the left presents the legends of all the items on the graphical part. By clicking on the arrow at the left of items (left window), it is possible to aggregate or expand the item. For example, the contextual elements (blue circles) are expanded and activities (pink ovals) not.

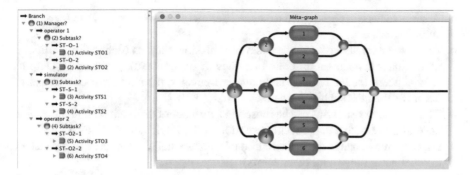

Fig. 5.3 Example of conceptual meta-graph

A turn consists of the selection of:

- The group member that will be the manager of the turn;
- The independent elementary subtask realized by the manager during the turn;
- The selection of the next manager and the concerned subtasks at the end of the turn.

The cyclic use of the contextual meta-graph associated with the shared context opens the possibility of backtracking into the group reasoning as well as the possibility of cycles for negotiation between two (or more) group members (**key point 22**).

In the CxG_1.0 version, practice development corresponds to a unique traversal of the contextual graph, which is directed, acyclic and with a series–parallel structure. The modeling of the practice is made jointly with its development. The practice is obtained by following a path from the input to the output of the contextual graph. In the CxG_2.0 version (with independent elementary subtasks instead of the contextualized task model), it is the CxG-based simulation of the group activity that corresponds to the cyclic traversal of the contextual meta-graph.

As a consequence, the group activity is developed jointly with its simultaneous modeling by assembling elementary subtasks as a sequence (**key point 23**).

The advantage is the possibility to dynamically represent simply complex structures of group activities like the contextualized task model for one actor. The inconvenience is the difficulty to give a simple explanation of the modeled group activity to the end-user.

The explicit consideration of the shared context with the contextual meta-graph opens the door to more options than before like [6]:

- The simulation can now be stopped at the end of any turn (with an action "RECIPIENT = <nil>").
- The use of simulation parameters introduces naturally the notion of loops for managing conflict, negotiation, alternative checking among actors and realizing a given subtask (or sequence of subtasks) in different contexts, thanks to the association of the contextual graph and the shared context.

- A same focus can be assigned to several actors (e.g. several reviewers for a paper submission).
- An elementary subtask may have several possible outputs (defined by particular contextual elements on different branches of the contextual subgraph). Outputs may concern the study of variants by the manager, the next actor or a subset of actors or the next subtask to realize.
- The elementary subtasks can be reused in a number of different combinations and several times with a unique representation at the implementation level.
- An actor may change the instantiation of a contextual element used in the task of another actor (or several other actors).

The dynamic modeling of the group activity development gives a new insight for addressing the focus of a unique actor with a "nonlinear" representation (thanks to the independent elementary tasks) of the actor activity, for example, checking first different alternatives by simulation (cyclic use of the contextual meta-graph for one actor) before making decision.

References

1. Brézillon, P., et al.: Modeling collaborative construction of an answer by contextual graphs. In: Proceedings of IPMU, Paris, France, pp. 11–13 (2006)
2. Karsenty, L., Brézillon, P.: Cooperative problem solving and explanation. Int. J. Expert Syst. Appl. **4**, 445–462 (1995)
3. Sarrazin, P., et al.: Goal orientations and conceptions of the nature of sport ability in children: a social cognitive approach. Br. J. Soc. Psychol. **35**, 399–414 (1996)
4. Benitez-Guerrero, E., et al.: Context-aware mobile collaborative systems: conceptual modeling and case study. Sensors **12**, 13491–13507 (2012)
5. Brézillon, P.: Some characteristics of context. In: Ali, M., Dapoigny, R. (eds.) Proceedings of IEA/AIE, Annecy, France, June 2006, Lecture Notes in Artificial Intelligence, vol. 4031, pp. 146–154. Springer Verlag (2006)
6. Garcia, K., Brézillon, P.: A contextual model of turns for group work. In: Christiansen, H., et al. (eds.) CONTEXT-15: Modeling and Using Context. Lecture Notes in Artificial Intelligence, vol. 9405, pp. 243–256. Springer (2015)
7. Brézillon, P.: Contextual modeling of group activity. In: Brézillon, P., et al. (eds.) CONTEXT 2017: Modeling and Using Context. Lecture Notes in Artificial Intelligence, vol. 10257, pp. 113–126. Springer International Publishing AG, Heldeiberg (2017)

Chapter 6
Discussion and Lessons Learned

This chapter regroups the lessons learned and the key points in the previous sections for a general discussion leading to the basis of context-based intelligent assistant systems. The key points identified previously in the text are met in Table 6.1 where we kept the original numbering and ordering of the key points in the different chapters. They are grouped in the following section in five general themes which are visualized by colors of the cells of the key point numbers in Table 6.1. Hereafter, this chapter discusses the contextual elements, first individually and second by themes. Based on the finer approach of contextual elements proposed in the first section and, thus, about context in general, the third section proposes a new insight on decisional levels in terms of context. The chapter ends on the use of context modeling and use in a future type of intelligent systems, namely the context-based intelligent assistant systems.

6.1 Lessons Learned on the Key Points of the Research

According to the focus of attention, we distinguish contextual knowledge and external knowledge (**key point 1**). Thus, conversely to what it is implicitly supposed in the literature, one cannot speak of context in an abstract way: Context and focus are interdependent (**key point 3**): Context constrains more the means to address the focus than the focus itself (**key point 4**).

Contextual elements (as expression of contextual knowledge) come from four sources, namely the actor, the focus, the situation and the local environment (**key point 5**). The sources being highly heterogeneous, it is better to consider contextual knowledge as a set of contextual elements, which may be instantiated in quantitative (e.g. a value) and qualitative (e.g. a name or another contextual element) ways. With respect to the focus of attention, contextual elements are partially ordered (**key point**

© The Author(s), under exclusive license to Springer Nature Switzerland AG 2023
P. Brézillon, *Research on Modeling and Using Context Over 25 Years*,
SpringerBriefs in Computer Science,
https://doi.org/10.1007/978-3-031-39338-9_6

Table 6.1 Key points on modeling and use of context (colors are discussed in Sect. 6.2)

Key point	Definition
1	The **focus of attention** allows to differentiate contextual knowledge and external knowledge
2	The **proceduralized context** is the part of the contextual knowledge that is used at one step of the focus
3	One cannot speak of context in abstract way: context and focus are interdependent
4	The means to implement the focus are as important as the result of the focus
5	There are four sources of **contextual elements**: the actor, the focus, the situation and the local environment
6	A contextual element and its instantiations must be treated separately
7	Contextual elements can be partially ordered with respect to the focus
8	A **practice** is a procedure contextualized in a specific context based on operational knowledge and experience of the actor
9	A **contextualized task model** represents all intertwined practices developed for a given focus
10	The contextualized task model is at the tactical level, while practice development is at the operational level
11	A **contextual element** is a pair {contextual node, recombination node} with exclusive branches between nodes expressing different practices
12	A **contextual graph** is a directed, acyclic series-parallel graph in which branches represent different strategies to achieve the focus
13	The **proceduralized context** is the sequence of contextual elements instantiated during the practice development
14	Practice and proceduralized context are built jointly
15	Contextual elements belong to the tactical level and instantiations to the operational level
16	The **experience base** is the sum of practices in a contextualized task model for a given focus of attention
17	The **shared-context** building is the first step of a group focus
18	Tasks of group members are decomposed in **independent elementary subtasks** and the task realization is a real-time and context-based generation of a sequence of subtasks
19	Elementary subtasks are realized successively in a cyclic application of the contextual graph
20	A **turn** is the traversal of the contextual graph for realizing the subtask of a group member and for updating the shared-context management for the next turn (subtask, groupmember)
21	A **CxG simulation** is a cyclic use of the contextual graph as long as the shared context is modified
22	The **contextual meta-graph** and its shared context allow to model dynamically nonlinear interactions among group member like negotiation
23	The development of the group activity in a contextual meta-graph is built jointly with its dynamic modeling as a sequence of elementary subtasks

7) and must be treated separately of their instantiations in the different contexts of application of the focus (**key point 6**).

A contextual element is modeled in the CxG formalism as a pair of a contextual node and a recombination node with exclusive branches between the nodes (**key point 11**). Branches correspond to different instantiations of the contextual element (i.e. different contexts) and several ways to address the focus step. Instantiation plays a role at the operational level (where is the practice development), while contextual elements define a structure on the practices at the conceptual level (**key point 15**), structure that is called contextualized task model previously.

The proceduralized context is the part of the contextual knowledge that is used in the focus (**key point 2**). It corresponds to the sequence of contextual elements that have been instantiated during the practice development (**key point 13**). The proceduralized context is built jointly with the practice development (**key point 14**).

A practice is a contextualization of a procedure in a specific context also based on actor's operational knowledge and experience (**key point 8**). Practices differ each other at contextual elements, and practices are intertwined in a contextualized task model (**key point 9**).

The contextualized task model and thus all the practices are at a conceptual level, while the development of practices is at the operational decisional level (**key point 10**). A contextual graph (the implementation of the task contextualized model) is an inclusive representation of all the practices developed by actors for addressing a focus in a variety of contexts.

A contextual graph is a directed, acyclic series–parallel graph where paths represent practices, the application of different strategies to achieve the focus (**key point 12**). Because a contextualized task model developed by actors contains all the practices developed in different contexts, a contextual graph is a representation of an **experience base** on a given focus of attention (**key point 16**).

The shared-context building on the fly ensures the coherency of the group members in their activity (**key point 17**). The contribution of each group member in the group's activity is assimilated to a set of independent elementary subtasks (**key point 18**) used in a cyclic application of the contextual graph (**key point 19**). A turn is the traversal of the contextual graph for realizing a subtask of a group member and for managing the shared context for the next turn (choice of the next subtask and group member) (**key point 20**).

CxG simulations are based on the cyclic use of the contextual graph as long as the shared context is modified (**key point 21**). The management of actors and their contributions to the group activity is implemented as a contextual meta-graph (and its shared context) that allows a dynamic modeling of nonlinear interactions among group member, like negotiation (**key point 22**). Thus, the focus progress (the development of the group activity) is expressed by this dynamic modeling of a sequence of elementary subtasks (**key point 23**).

6.2   Lessons Learned on a Grouping of the Key Points

These key points can be grouped in five themes:

1.   Context and focus of attention (**key points 1, 3, 4** with a yellow background);
2.   Proceduralized context (**key points 2, 13, 14** with an orange background);
3.   Contextual elements (**key points 5, 6, 7, 11, 15** with a green background);
4.   CxG_1.0 version of the CxG formalism (**key points 8, 9, 10, 12, 16** with a dark blue background);
5.   CxG_2.0 version of the CxG formalism (**key points 17, 18, 19, 20, 21, 22, 23** with a clear blue background).

The themes correspond to a progressive refinement of the research from general ideas to the software CxG_1.0 and CxG_2.0, which have been used in our real-world applications. The concept of experience base represents for us a new field of investigation by considering all the focuses in a given domain (e.g. the exploitation of a subway line).

The first theme "context and focus of attention" defines our conceptual framework that proposes a modeling of context for an effective use in real-world applications. This was possible by an operational definition of context that points out the interdependency of context and focus and the application of general concepts like operational knowledge and context, the latter allowing to concretize the role of sources of context like the actor, focus, situation and actor's knowledge.

The second theme "proceduralized context" illustrates how the contextual elements intervening in the focus are progressively instantiated during the practice development to finally get the proceduralized context, which appears as a kind of evidence of the contextual nature of explanation introduced by Karsenty and Brézillon [1].

The third theme "contextual elements" gives consistency to the concept of context as objective elements (but possible subjective instantiations). Contextual elements are: defined at a conceptual level, instantiated at the operational level and used in a particular representation at the implementation level through the CxG formalism.

The representation of contextual elements as pairs {contextual node, recombination node} imposes a logic of representation such as a contextual element includes another contextual element on one of its branches (as nested dolls) without partial overlapping. Contextual elements define the fixed structure of a contextualized task model, and instantiations constitute the variable part (the practice development for addressing a particular focus), variable part depending on the four sources of context.

The fourth and fifth themes concern the CxG representation formalism in the two successive versions CxG_1.0 and CxG_2.0, according to the number of actors that intervene for addressing the focus of attention (one or several). For one actor (CxG_1.0 version), the working context is in the actor's head and thus not made fully explicit. For this reason, the CxG_1.0 software is used considering that all the contextual elements in the contextual graph constitute the explicit part of the working context of the actor addressing the focus, and the hidden part of the working context stays in actor's head. The contextualized task model implemented as a contextual graph is enriched progressively by the actor (or several actors).

The key difference between the CxG_1.0 and CxG_2.0 versions corresponds to the representation of the focus of attention on either a (unique) contextualized task model that meets all the known practices or on a breakdown of the contextualized task model in independent elementary subtasks that are dynamically combinable in different ways including in the reasoning cycles and unexpected practice sequences. Another difference between the two versions concerns the context management associated with the focus.

The contextual graphs representation formalism relies only on four elements, namely the action, the contextual element, the activity and the executive structure of independent activities (ESIA). The version CxG-2.0 of the CxG formalism was implemented for a focus concerning the activity of a group of actors. Conversely to the working context in CxG_1.0, the building of the shared context and the development of the group's activity in parallel suppose a specific management of actors and of their contribution to the group's activity (allocation of the role of manager to the actor responsible of the subtask realized during the turn). Thus, the changes from CxG_1.0 to CxG_2.0 concern:

- The management of actor interactions with a shared context between the working contexts and the proceduralized context;
- A task decomposition in independent elementary subtasks;
- A cyclic traversing of the contextual graph (the notion of turn) for realizing each elementary subtask instead of the contextualized task model.

In the CxG_2.0 software, the shared context is totally visible for sharing purposes (it can be considered as the intersection of all the working contexts of the group members).

Another difference between CxG_1.0 and CxG_2.0 versions is the cyclic use of the contextual graph that allows, at the conceptual level, to introduce the checking of alternatives and possibilities of negotiation among others and, at the implementation level, the introduction of a function of simulation (CxG simulation) in the software.

A third difference between CxG-1.0 and CxG_2.0 versions concerns the viewpoints that are expressed. CxG_1.0 version corresponds to an external viewpoint on the result obtained once the focus is reached, while CxG_2.0 version is for an internal viewpoint on how the focus is reached. In the CxG_2.0 version, the explicit part of the working context of CxG_1.0 version becomes the shared context that is built jointly with the focus progress. It implies that the focus of attention can be put in question at any time.

6.3   Context and Decisional Levels

Decision-making presents four interdependent decisional levels, namely policy, strategy, tactic and operation. For Canton [2], policies establish the broad framework for decisions and action, generally expressed in qualitative, conditional or general way.

The strategy defines the direction in which the organization must go to stay in the policy by examining long-range implications of the event, determining long-term goals and objectives and establishing priorities that will guide operational response.

The tactic tackles the overall response to the event by coordinating all the means, resources and public information. It concerns actions, procedures, schedules, each element being selected according to the picture given by the strategy. This abstracted description can be applied in any of a large class of situations.

Operation leads to contextualize the tactical decision by selecting operational instances of the elements from the four sources of context (i.e. the actor, the task, the situation and the environment) to respond directly to the impacts of an event at the field level. An application of these concepts in the domain of car driving is given in Brézillon et al. [3].

Decisional levels constitute the framework of decision-making. Each level determines planning assumptions, level of detail and resources required. The two upper levels (policy and strategy) constitute a stable part that commits the decision-making to the long term, while the two lower levels (tactical and operational) correspond to the dynamic (and short term) part of the decision-making and correspond to the domain where context intervenes. Roughly, the stable part defines the general referential, and the dynamic part defines the contextual dressing of this decision-making referential.

For example, I want to invite friends for my birthday. I decide first to organize a diner (policy level), second to invite them in a restaurant and not at home (strategy level), third I opt for a Japanese restaurant (tactical level), and fourth I choose the Japanese restaurant that is close from my home (operational level). Each decisional level is a specialization of the decisional level just above; however, the two latter can be put in question more easily (e.g. several invited persons do not like Japanese food and another type of restaurant must be found).

For the purpose of this monograph (modeling and use of context), we made several choices at the policy and strategy levels, like the four sources of contextual elements (actor, focus, situation and environment), the choice of an operational definition of context, the emphasis on the relationships between context, operational knowledge and reasoning and the choice of a context-based representation formalism. All along the chapters we showed the development of several concepts during our research operate simultaneously at the tactical and operational decisional levels. For including the two first levels not directly concerned (i.e. the policy and the strategy levels), we consider modeling and using context at the conceptual and the operational levels, the conceptual level covering the levels of policy, strategy and tactical decisional.

This puts some light on the duality like procedure vs. practice and mental representation vs. mental model because they address the same problem at two different levels. We also have this distinction with contextual graph and practices at the conceptual level and instantiation of contextual elements and practice development at the operational level.

In the TACTIC project, the "tactical expert" and the "operational expert" in the TACTIC project are able to have the same focus, each with his own mental representation and different mental models of it.

In the SART project for the subway, the responsible of a subway line (the tactical actor) says to the driver of the train (the operational actor) "Make your train empty of travelers". For the former it is a simple action, while the latter faces a complex activity (make an announcement in the train, stop at the next station, etc.).

This two-level framework makes possible to provide a more precise definition of the concepts that we have introduced in this monograph by placing them on the conceptual level or the operational level like we do initially as shown in Fig. 3.1. For example, the contextualized task model is at the conceptual level and is implemented as a contextual graph at the operational level. It is also the difference we introduced between the mental representation and mental models at the conceptual level and the mental model building at the operational level. This will be the topic of another book because the simplistic distinction conceptual level and operational level are insufficient.

6.4 Context-Based Intelligent Assistant Systems (CIASs)

Context-based intelligent systems *contextualize* the methods to use in the situation at hand. Two approaches to context-based systems generally are evoked in AI, formal and pragmatic approaches [4]. Formal approaches concern formal properties and relationships between a set of discrete contexts and only try to solve real problems, while pragmatic approaches focus first on solving real-world problems and then on abstracting general principles from what has been done.

One research line concerns context-based reasoning based on actors' experiences, namely *joint cognitive systems* (JCSs; [5]). Here, the focus was on the complementary competence and skills of the human and the system with respect to problem solving, especially their cognitive asymmetry. The line of reasoning in a JCS, developed during problem solving, is a co-construction of the system and the actor.

Explanations are an intrinsic part of the construction [6]. Unfortunately, context was not made explicit in JCSs. AI systems aim to understand actor(s) through their decisions, actions and behaviors, not from some abstract actor models or profiles from a library.

Such systems called *intelligent assistant systems* (IASs) operate in conjunction with an actor to accomplish a given task, for example, systems that handle subway incidents, medical diagnostic assistants or pedagogical activities.

IASs' knowledge of the context is often sparse. It may rely on location (GPS), internet-based services (weather, etc.) and expected properties of the task, as well as an actor profile based on statistical considerations and augmented or selected with the help of available sensors (e.g. biometric sensors for identification or determining physiological state). However, most IASs lack any attention to the full panoply of facts, knowledge and detail that is the total context in which IASs and actors cooperate.

Among these AI systems that use context as a central component of their behavior, we are concerned by *context-based intelligent assistant systems,* CIASs [7]. The actor stays the decision-maker during interaction with a CIAS that mainly proposes satisfying alternatives and may justify them, including recalling relevant points from previous interactions. A CIAS is a decision support system for actors that have a high level of expertise in a domain which is not well-known or too complex. Actors' expertise is highly compiled contextual knowledge built mainly by experience and is generally used in a decision-making process leading to a critical and definitive decision.

There are several consequences. First, the CIAS must be able to follow what experts are doing and how they are doing it and anticipate their needs. This means that the system must have some model of the experts' reasoning (e.g. experience bases). The system also needs to be a competent secretary, fixing all the simple problems the experts encounter by itself and preparing dossiers on complex situations to enable the experts to make their own decisions. The CIAS's line of reasoning relies on human experts' reasoning as represented in a contextualized task model.

The CIASs developed in the CxG formalism offer the possibility to model reasoning as context-based simulation. A CxG simulation corresponds to a bottom-up model (the model is built jointly with its use and instantiation of contextual elements can be modified). In a CxG simulation, the shared context evolves dynamically during practice development. A practice is built progressively by the CxG simulator.

In that sense, a CxG simulation is a particular type of simulation. The main tool of a CIAS is a CxG simulator that allows real-time decision-making because it is then possible to account for unpredicted events, thanks to explicitly modeling context as contextual elements that cover the actor, the task realization, the working situation and the local environment with its available resources.

Simulation abilities allow anticipation of outcomes even when there is a lack of comprehensive a priori planning. The system determines how to behave according to the predictions, that is, anticipated future states that may affect its present states. It also allows to explore different dynamics of reasoning: validation, checking alternatives, replaying a reasoning sequence in different contexts, explanation, etc. CxG simulations may propose the generation of explanations for predictions, making the CIAS an effective decision support system.

In addition to CxG simulation abilities, a CIAS also requires several other abilities:

- **Explanation**. Explanation is a means of developing a shared context between the CIAS and the actor that co-construct the explanation based on the current context of the focus. Explanations concern the context of using the knowledge and reasoning. The proceduralized context, which is associated with a practice, provides an ordered sequence of instantiated contextual elements that can be detailed to explain the rationale behind the development of the practice. There are different types of context-based explanations that are possible thanks to the real-time development of the practice that is simulated, like visual explanations, dynamic explanations, actor-based explanations, context-based explanations, micro- and macro-explanations, real-time explanations and explanations that can be combined in different ways such as visual and dynamic explanations for presenting future alternatives and abandoned options [8].

- **Browsing**. Browsing differs from simulation with respect to time in the decision-making process. A browser works at a tactical level where time and action execution are not considered explicitly. For example, duration of an action does not matter because the execution of the action is not considered, while the lack of resource blocks an action and matters for a simulation. It is more a qualitative comparison than an effective development of the practice in the context at hand. The focus is more on the realizability of the task in a given context than its effective realization.

- **Knowledge acquisition**. A CIAS cannot have all the needed knowledge at design time, and the system may fail by lack of knowledge; the actor enriches the base of experience with a new practice where the knowledge is provided in its context of use. Incremental knowledge acquisition relies on the fact that actors' knowledge is essentially a justification (i.e. explanation) of their judgment in that context. This ability is intrinsic to CIASs.

- **Learning**. A learning tool is particularly important for situation in which there is a discrepancy between a practice that is developed by an actor and the system's expectations based on its experience base. This may occur because the actor selects either a new instantiation for a known contextual element (learning by assimilation) or a new contextual element that has kept the same instantiation during all practice development (and thus was not considered in the experience base) and has now to be considered (learning by accommodation). It is a kind of training of the CIAS by actors.

- **Training**. The CIAS also may be a trainer for actors not quite familiar with practices for realizing a task as described in the experience base of the CIAS. The training here consists of explaining the elements used during a practice development, especially contextual elements, their instantiations in the proceduralized context and the variants abandoned (i.e. the other branches between a contextual node and the recombination node).

- **Communication**. Communication is a key ability of a system for actor–CIAS interaction during their joint problem solving. The communication component must be able to handle interruptions, reorient as needed and resume work at any point by using the other abilities for explaining, learning practices and acquiring knowledge.

All these abilities, explanation, browsing, incremental knowledge acquisition and learning communication are integrated in context-based intelligent assistant systems and operated on the same experience base (produced by actors) as a shared medium for them. As a consequence, knowledge acquisition and learning appear as the two sides of a same ability.

References

1. Karsenty, L., Brézillon, P.: Cooperative problem solving and explanation. Int. J. Expert Syst. Appl. **4**, 445–462 (1995)
2. Canton, L.G.: Emergency Management: Concepts and Strategies for Effective Programs. J. Wiley & Sons Inc (2007)
3. Brézillon, P., et al.: Context-based methodology for decision making: application for car driving. Int. J. Decision Syst. Technol. **1**(3), 1–20 (2009)
4. Turner, R.M., Brézillon, P.: Toward pragmatic context-based systems. In: Brézillon, P., Turner, R.M. (eds) Modeling and Using Context in Action, pp. 53–86. ISTE Science Publishing Ltd (2022)
5. Woods, D.D.: Cognitive technologies: the design of joint human–machine cognitive systems. AI Mag. **6**(4), 86–92 (1985)
6. Brézillon, P., Abu-Hakima, S.: Using knowledge in its context: report on the IJCAI-93 Workshop. AI Mag. Spring **16**(1), 87–91 (1995)
7. Brézillon, P.: Chap. 07: context-centered tools for intelligent assistant systems. In: Brézillon, P., Gonzalez, A. (eds.) Context in Computing: A Cross-Disciplinary Approach for Modeling the real World Through Contextual Reasoning, pp. 97–110. Springer, NY (2014)
8. Brézillon, P.: Explaining for contextualizing and contextualizing for explaining. In: ExaCt 2008: Proceedings of 3rd International Workshop on Explanation-Aware Computing. CEUR Workshop Proceedings, ISSN 1613-0073. Patras, Greece (2008). https://CEUR-WS.org/Vol-391/000 10001.pdf

Chapter 7
Conclusion

The approach presented in this paper is ascribed in the realm of AI that is based on separation of representation and use of knowledge in a given implementation with an emphasis on the modeling of context for real-world use. We consider a stricter separation of representation and use than in previous works on the web: On the one hand, knowledge is not "tailored" for entering the representation formalism, and in the other hand, the formalism does not focus on some (more or less hidden) restrictive goals for use of the knowledge.

For example, the production-rule formalism only accepts declarative knowledge under the expression "If <conditions> then <conclusion>", and the introduction of procedural knowledge of different natures generates a syntax/semantics confusion like screening clauses and rule packets for controlling this procedural knowledge.

The CxG representation formalism has been used with success in twenty very different real-world applications because the modeling of the actors' expertise is made at a tactical level (i.e. domain level), and its use is at an operational level (i.e. our application level). The CxG formalism has no hidden methods like the control of the firing of rules by the inference engine in expert systems where it is the designer that orders the rules to check for firing a rule before another one.

The "human dimension of knowledge" plays a central role in the acquisition and representation of the expert knowledge that is highly contextualized. The CxG representation formalism only has four "generic" entities (action, contextual element, activity and ESIA) for modeling domain knowledge and reasoning at the tactical level and after for using it at the operational level (where context is expressed explicitly through the instantiations of the contextual elements). Thus, the CxG formalism proposes a uniform representation of knowledge, reasoning and context.

At the implementation level (where are software CxG_1.0 and CxG_2.0), complex behaviors result from various combinations of a small number of reasoning units (i.e. the contextual elements where a method is selected according to the instantiation of

P. Brézillon, *Research on Modeling and Using Context Over 25 Years*,
SpringerBriefs in Computer Science,
https://doi.org/10.1007/978-3-031-39338-9_7

the contextual element). In addition, the CxG_2.0 version uses a contextual meta-graph based on independent elementary subtasks instead of a global modeling of the tasks of group members. Here is the real separation between representation and use (at tactical and operational levels).

The "hard kernel" of our approach is the explicit modeling of context as contextual elements that leads to a homogeneous view on how a class of AI systems can become context-based intelligent systems. This book presents a discussion on the particular requirements for the special class of context-based intelligent systems that interested us, namely context-based intelligent assistant systems (CIASs), the differences with context-based intelligent autonomous agents (CIAAs) being discussed elsewhere [1].

The goal is not a direct discovery like for machine and deep learning, but a reuse and an extension of the human experience. For deep learning, the goal would not be to accumulate contextual knowledge (infinite dimension of context), but to be able to identify in the situation and the environment the contextual elements that are relevant in a context at hand for a robot to accomplish its task and develop its contextualized task model in a kind of a "modeling by acting". The CxG formalism provides powerful experience bases that can be served as basis for deep learning in order to complete the known practices.

This monograph sums up 25 years of research on how to model and use context in twenty real-world applications on a spectrum from technology-centered (SEPT, SART) to human-centered (e.g. FlexMIm) applications, that is, from well-defined domains to more fuzzy ones. Real-world applications impose strong requirements and imply the rejection of simplifying assumptions: The operator in a crisis unit and the surgeon in an emergency room have to rapidly make a decision that will be definitive. Thus, an answer of a system to a question asked by such actors like "Well, in 80% of the cases, the solution is…" is not acceptable, because the decision is made in a precise context that constrains that urgent decision-making.

Although the CxG formalism has been applied successfully in several fields (e.g. medicine, transportation, business management and military operations), there are some limitations. Actors have difficulty following the development of a specific practice in the contextual graph (especially in the CxG_2.0 version) and to make the decision that is associated with it. Often, experts need to quickly identify the right practice that matches the specific context at hand and the resulting sequences of actions to execute (especially in emergency situations). Thus, experts evaluate first the proceduralized context corresponding to the situation at hand to make immediate decision (e.g. handle an incident in the subway) and, second, to infer the type of object of the reasoning corresponding to the content of a given practice.

An object involved with reasoning can be either a physical object (e.g. a digital image in medicine) or a cognitive object (e.g. a diagnosis). We propose to actors a conversion of the contextual graph in a practice tree representation (and not a decision tree representation) for allowing a fast understandability of the focus by actors with an explicit proceduralized context and of the corresponding sequence of actions to perform [2]. The practice tree representation, in the CxG formalism, expresses the high level of automaticity through a single-step retrieval of actions from memory [3]. It is not a simple decision tree. Klein and Calderwood [4] show that decision-making may proceed directly from recognized situations to predefined actions. Both accounts point to a situation where skilled knowledge is accessed and utilized in ways that do not necessarily lend themselves to easy verbalization.

The consideration of several focuses in a domain may lead to a set of experience bases that can be assembled in a unique repository (e.g. incident solving on a subway line is one of the focuses that concerns the exploitation of a subway line). We illustrated with the SART project that the incident "Ill traveler in a train" is related to another incident "Traveler on tracks" through contextual elements because they rely on the same knowledge and contextual elements. At the level of the contextualized task model, this interdependency may be formalized more precisely through shared activities or contextual elements.

Interestingly, the CxG_2.0 version of the CxG formalism developed for group activity stays applicable to a unique actor with the interests of:

- Modeling nonlinear reasoning. A nonlinear exploitation of a task realization or activity, while the task model stays "linear";
- Integration of the environment state. The actor may change his/her mind during practice development when an unexpected event occurs (e.g. the actor selects an object and later discovers that the object is not adapted to the objective or not available);
- Simulation. The actor can replay several times a particular subtask for checking different hypothesis (i.e. different contexts) before making decision;
- Exploration of a decision tree. The actor can backtrack in his/her reasoning.

Context is strongly associated with knowledge and reasoning about a real-world focus. In some sense, context has multiple aspects like object (knowledge) and process (reasoning). Context intervenes more on the nature of the knowledge than on the knowledge itself: Knowledge is contextual or not depending on the focus. However, it is not sufficient to just say that for modeling and using context. The results of this research are not limited to the initial focuses we considered, that is, the task realization, decision-making and problem solving.

The CxG simulation can be used for other "context-dependent" focuses of attention like evaluation of employees, hiring of candidates based on simulation of real-world conditions, training and self-training of apprentices based on good as well as bad practices drawing of the enterprise, statistics over actors applying a practice as well as all the practices developed by a given actor, on the practices the most used in a contextualized task model (identify the "best practice" for a given focus) and debriefing on a focus addressing.

The behavior of actors realizing the same task (in parallel or sequentially) can be studied and compared by simulation of their task realizations to determine, say, those that develop safe or risky practices (and also for statistics and hiring candidates).

The choice (not dependent of us) of the applications in very different domains and disciplines was essential, and the results obtained during this research depend on the projects and applications used during these 25 years. It is possible that with other applications, the research will have deviate toward other results (or none).

References

1. Turner, R.M., Brézillon, P.: Toward pragmatic context-based systems. In: Brézillon, P., Turner, R.M. (eds.) Modeling and Using Context in Action. ISTE Science Publishing Ltd, pp. 53–86 (2022)
2. Garcia, K., Brezillon, P.: Model vizualization: combining context-based graph and tree representations. Expert Syst. Appl. **99**(1), 103–114 (2018)
3. Logan, G.D.: Automaticity, resources and memory: theoretical controversies and practical implications. Hum. Factors **30**(5), 583–598 (1988)
4. Klein, G.A., Calderwood, R.: Decision models: some lessons from the field. IEEE Trans. Syst. Man Cybern. **21**(5), 1018–1026 (1991)

Printed in the United States
by Baker & Taylor Publisher Services